ENTREPRENEURSHIP & PROJECT MANAGEMENT

DR. MUKTA GOYAL

Copyright © Dr. Mukta Goyal
All Rights Reserved.

Contents

Preface

The process of turning an idea into a business is complicated and sophisticated. To operate profitably in a high-risk environment, necessitates the identification and verification of numerous facts, the elimination of guesswork, and an emphasis on control in the expenditure of limited resources (cash, time, and people).

Entrepreneurship is an important factor in a country's industrial development. It is an entrepreneur's primary trade. Entrepreneurs differ in terms of their level and quality of entrepreneurship. However, certain agent determinants have an impact on the development progress and growth of entrepreneurship.

Proper project management entails real-time direction, coordination, reassessment, and reconfiguration. The entrepreneur must complete the work on time, on budget, and to the satisfaction of the customers. This results in exceptional performance and profit for the company and its investors. The ability of the management team to complete tasks on time, at the lowest possible cost, and with maximum efficiency and effectiveness is the primary characteristic of a successful business opportunity.

The essence of success is meticulous planning and preparation. The founder takes on the roles of planner, designer, implementer, scheduler, monitor, procurer, and director. There is a critical need for formal project management tools to help entrepreneurs.

The one-of-a-kind book was created for high-performing entrepreneurs with the potential to be effective project managers/entrepreneurs. It strives to provide students with a clear view of Entrepreneurship and Project Management.

The ability of entrepreneurs to start businesses is influenced by the cultures of nations around the world.

Dr Mukta Goyal

ENTREPRENEUR: PHILOSOPHY OF ENTREPRENEURSHIP, DIFFERENCE BETWEEN SELF–EMPLOYMENT AND ENTREPRENEURSHIP & DIFFERENT FORMS OF BUSINESS ORGANIZATION

Introduction

Entrepreneurship

Entrepreneurship is the process of creating or extracting economic value. According to this definition, entrepreneurship is defined as change, generally involving risk beyond what is normally encountered when starting a business, and may include values other than monetary ones.

An entrepreneur is a person who creates and/or invests in one or more businesses, bearing the majority of the risks and reaping the majority of the rewards. Entrepreneurship refers to the process of starting a business. The entrepreneur is frequently regarded as an innovator, a source of new ideas, goods, services, and business/or procedures.

"Entrepreneur"

A person who generates money by creating or running enterprises, particularly when taking financial risks, is known as an 'Entrepreneur', or an entrepreneur is a person who starts a new firm and bears most of the risks while reaping the majority of the benefits. Entrepreneurship refers to the process of starting a business. The entrepreneur is frequently portrayed as a pioneer, a provider of novel ideas, products, services, and/or business processes.

Entrepreneurs are critical to any economy because they have the ability and initiative to anticipate requirements and bring good new ideas to market. Entrepreneurship that succeeds in taking on the risks of starting a business is rewarded with revenues, fame, and chances for continued expansion. Failure of an entrepreneur results in losses and a lower market presence for individuals concerned.

Entrepreneurial Characteristics

You may wonder whether the term "entrepreneur" simply means "a person who starts a business and is willing to risk loss in order to make money," or whether it also implies foresight and innovation. The answer, perhaps unsatisfactorily, is that it can go either way.

Since at least the middle of the 18th century, when it appeared in a translation of the King of Prussia's instructions for his generals ("... if the country happens not to abound in forage, you must agree with some Entrepreneur for the quantity required.") During the nineteenth century, It was also used to describe a go-between or someone who performs any type of activity (as opposed to just a business).

When applied to an independent business owner in the early twentieth century, the term entrepreneur appears to have taken on the connotation of a go-getter, a quality that may also be found in the phrase entrepreneurial spirit, which began being used around the same time.

- An entrepreneur is a person who accepts the risk of establishing a new business enterprise.
- An entrepreneur establishes a company to carry out their business idea, which combines capital and labour to generate goods or services for profit.
- Entrepreneurship is high-risk, but it may also be high-rewarding, since it contributes to economic prosperity, growth, and innovation.
- Obtaining finance is critical for entrepreneurs: SBA loans and crowdsourcing are two options for funding.
- The method entrepreneurs file and pay taxes is determined by the form of their firm.

Concept and nature, scope and philosophy of entrepreneurship:

Entrepreneurship is defined as the capacity and willingness to create, organise, and run a firm, including all of its risks, in order to make a profit. The most visible form of entrepreneurship is the establishment of new firms.

An entrepreneur is a person responsible for setting up a business or an enterprise. He has the initiative, skill for innovation and who looks for high achievements. He is a catalytic agent of change and works for the good of people. He puts up new green field projects that create wealth, opens up many employment opportunities and leads to growth of other sectors.

Entrepreneur Types

- **Social Entrepreneurs:** Individuals who engage in innovative solutions to social issues are referred to as social entrepreneurs. This type of entrepreneur adopts a style that allows him or her to create and sustain social values.
- **Serial Business Owners:** Serial entrepreneurs start several businesses in the hopes of running one of them for a long time. They are primarily high-risk takers with a lot of extraordinary ideas who are not always involved in a career with a specific company or business.
- **Lifestyle Entrepreneurs:** Individuals who profit from their personal interests. He/she showcased their lifestyle at every opportunity. The lifestyle entrepreneur creates a business that they are passionate about and grows it into a long-term, residual, and continuous income.

In short, the different *concepts of entrepreneurship* are as follows:

1. The Risk-Taking Concept: This is the most well-known and well-liked concept. "Entrepreneurship is the ability to take unrestricted risks."

This has proven that the entrepreneur must bear a variety of risks in order to start and run a new business.

These dangers are linked to variations in time and price volatility. Entrepreneurship as a concept is fraught with dangers. Furthermore, they have made a minor distinction between risk and uncertainty in their explanation.

"Uncertainty bears risk, which can neither be forecast nor covered," according to this.

2. A novel concept: According to this definition, an entrepreneur in a developed economy is "someone whose parents have created something new in the economy."

Entrepreneurial innovation is a specific tool.

Entrepreneurship has been defined under this idea as the adoption of numerous innovations in industries, such as new manufacturing systems or techniques, new products, new markets, new marketing tactics, new raw material qualities, new packaging, and new mixing procedures.

As a result, this is considered a contemporary entrepreneurship notion.

3. The Concept of Managerial Skill: Scholars who endorse this idea have redefined entrepreneurship as the ability to manage.

Entrepreneurship can be defined as the ability to inspect, control, and direct.

In the same way, entrepreneurship as a managerial skill, as well as the ability to bear risks.

4. Concept of Creativity and Leadership: Entrepreneurship, according to this definition, is a creative activity and a function of progressive leadership.

Similarly, entrepreneurship is the ability to expand an institution's resources, develop human capability, engage in creative activities, and coordinate new ideas.

He believes that new ideas occur as a result of creativity, which may then be put to economic use by effective leadership.

Creativity activities also expand due to high-level entrepreneurship.

5. Professional Approach: Entrepreneurship is now recognised as a professional notion by modern management professionals.

They believe that education and training can help to develop entrepreneurship.

Education and training can help you build managerial skills, and education and training can also help you create an entrepreneurial mind set.

As a result, governments and private groups run a variety of training programmes to help people develop their entrepreneurial skills.

6. Concept of Organization and Coordination: Entrepreneurship is the part of the economy that organises and coordinates numerous production sources. Entrepreneurship is defined as the "capacity to organise a business."

7. A Business-Oriented Approach: Entrepreneurship is defined as an individual's business-oriented entrepreneurial attitude that motivates people to become entrepreneurs, engage in business thinking, develop strategies and programmes, and start businesses.

8. The Concept of High Achievement Capacity: Entrepreneurship is a high-achievement capability idea that requires the ability to innovate and make decisions in the face of danger.

Two aspects of entrepreneurship are addressed in the assumption:

1) Ability to complete work using the most up-to-date manner.

2) The ability to make decisions in the face of uncertainty.

He has also assumed that a man becomes an entrepreneur because of his inspiration for high-level achievements.

9. The Idea of a Result-Oriented Concept: In the present day, entrepreneurship is referred to as result-oriented, according to this philosophy.

What matters now is the outcome, not the efforts made toward achieving the goals or the amount of hard work put in.

Only those who succeed in attaining their objectives are considered entrepreneurs in the business world.

10. Personality, Identity or Role Transformation Process Concept: Entrepreneurship is not only to adopt new works and behaviour, but it is also the transformation of personality and to establish a new identity through that.

The definition of entrepreneurship is discussed, as well as the nature of its underpinnings. The concept of an entrepreneurial mind set is discussed, as well as its characteristics and ramifications for the impoverished. The nature of entrepreneurship as a process is studied, as well as the particular elements of the stages of this process for a person in poverty. Entrepreneurship is defined as a turbulent, unexpected, and often chaotic journey in which the individual creates reality as it unfolds.

Entrepreneurship is about new possibilities – it is about acting on a dream, and concerns what is possible with hard work and imagination.

Entrepreneurship's Purpose (*Scope of entrepreneurship*):

The small-scale business provides ample opportunity for the expansion of entrepreneurial activities. Rather than producing a product, an entrepreneur has excellent opportunities and great scope in selling services. When the size of the small business is small and limited, the entrepreneur can achieve better results. As a result, small businesses have higher productivity, higher performance, and lower labour turnover.In a developing country like India, the potential for entrepreneurship is enormous. The country's unemployment rate is steadily increasing. There's also the issue of underemployment to consider. According to the Labour Bureau, the employment rate was 5% in 2015-2016, the highest in the previous five years. Women have a greater rate of 8.7% than men, who had a rate of 4.3 percent. The anticipated unemployment rate was 5%, according to the 5th all-India annual employment-unemployment survey conducted under Usual Principal Status (UPS). The solution is to promote the country's entrepreneurial activities.

Prospects in the Industrial Sector

Small-scale businesses play an important role in the industrial sector. In 1998, they accounted for 40 per cent of total industrial production. The primary goals underlying small-scale development are to increase the supply of manufactured goods, promote the capital report, develop domestic entrepreneurial capacities and skills, and create more job opportunities.

Of course, there are compelling reasons for young people to pursue this career path.

- People are ambitious and want to be in charge of their own destiny.
- There is the potential for increased profits.
- The country is grappling with an unemployment problem, and alternative professional opportunities are few.
- is dedicated to fostering entrepreneurship on a bigger scale.

In its report, the Planning Commission strongly advocated self-employment to redirect the unemployed youth in the direction of creating employment opportunities for 10 million individuals. The Indian government, state governments, and numerous national and regional organisations are all working to foster entrepreneurship through various plans and programmes. Here, I'd like to call attention to the Maharashtra Economic Development Council (MEDC), which has focused on entrepreneurship development through research and training. It has also led in the emergence of a new dimension. Entrepreneurship has become a part of the management college curriculum. Workshops and seminars on entrepreneurship have begun to be organised by apex institutions. As a result, the country's overall entrepreneurship development movement has begun and is projected to gain significant traction in the coming years.

Difference between self-employment and entrepreneurship:

An entrepreneur and a self-employed individual may share the commonality of owning a firm, but beyond that, their paths diverge dramatically.

We can see how these two positions intersect as business owners in the diagram below. However, when we take a closer look, we can see that the self-employed are the business, whereas an entrepreneur runs a business.

Self-Employed - Rather than working for an employer, one works for oneself as a freelancer or as the owner of a firm.

Entrepreneur - A person who establishes and operates a firm or businesses while taking on larger than average financial risks in order to accomplish so is known as an entrepreneur.

Typically, the majority of business owners fall into the "self-employed" group. They begin with a skill or combination of skills and discover that an opportunity to produce money presents itself. This is where the business crash course begins. From insurance and licences to accounting and marketing, many business owners quickly become suffocated by the seemingly endless hours required to keep the business afloat.

While many people still term themselves "business owners," they often have all of the responsibilities of an employee. This jumble of responsibilities might put the company's prosperity in jeopardy. Working anywhere from two to ten jobs, the self-employed are frequently overworked, underpaid, and lucky to have a few days off per year.

An entrepreneur, on the other hand, is all about risk and return. They look for new and innovative ways to succeed and move on to their next project. While the businesses may be interesting, the enthusiasm of the start-up and the desire to see something succeed is what motivates them every day. Once they have everything in place for the future, they may decide to sell the firm or start a new one.

Entrepreneurs:
-Flexible
-Creative
-Confident
-Passionate
Self-Employed:
-Hard Working
-Goal Oriented
-Quality Conscious
-Good Communicator

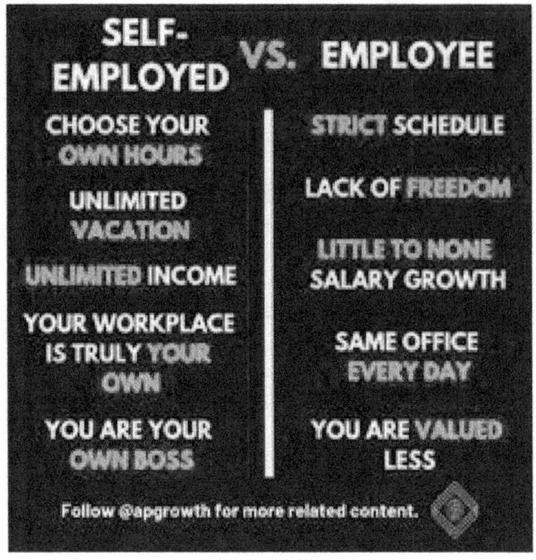

Source: Pinterest

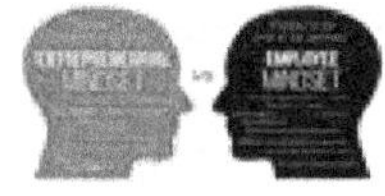

Source: Proverbsexplained

Importance of entrepreneurship and self-employment in our country: The young population of India, which is rapidly expanding, is adaptive and future-oriented. However, just one out of every twenty persons has got any skill training, compared to three out of every four people in Germany who are ready to work. In India, talent development has rarely kept up with technological advancement. So far, skill training has not had the impact that policymakers and government officials had hoped for. According to a survey released on February 27th by the Centre for Monitoring Indian Economy, there are roughly 31 million unemployed Indians looking for work presently, the largest number since October 2016. (CMIE). There are still some obstacles to overcome in order to realise its full potential and develop a trained global workforce.

As a result, self-employment and entrepreneurship are one of the solutions. In developing countries, self-employment is becoming more widely recognised as a viable source of income. It eases the pressure on employment generation and promotes self-sufficiency with limited resources. Self-employment and entrepreneurship have the potential to regularly create jobs and reduce the number of unemployed people.

A variety of central and state government programmes have emphasised the importance of self-employment in the framework of the sustainable development goals — creating jobs, stimulating economic growth and innovation, improving social conditions, and tackling environmental concerns. UnLtd India has been working in Mumbai with a number of social entrepreneurs from various sectors who have established organisations that promote self-employment and entrepreneurship in India's rural and urban areas.

Entrepreneurs are vital in market economies because they can act as the driving force behind the country's economic growth. They create new employment by developing new products and services, which leads to an acceleration of economic development.

Profession is an approach to making one's vocation. Self employment is likewise a vocation since one might utilize oneself in business or in assistance exercises and acquire one's job. With developing joblessness and absence of sufficient open positions, self employment has become extremely critical.

- Advantage of Small Businesses

Small-scale business enjoys a few upper hands over huge scope business. It tends to be handily begun, and requires limited quantity of capital venture. The self employment including exercises on a limited scale is a decent option in contrast to huge scope business which has brought different wrongs like ecological contamination, improvement of ghettos, double-dealing of laborers, etc.

- Preference over Wage Employment

In self employment there is no restriction of profit similarly as with wage business. In self employment one can involve one's ability for own advantage. The choices can be taken rapidly and advantageously. This large number of variables go about areas of strength for as for self employment to be liked over wage business.

- Developing the spirit of Entrepreneurship

Entrepreneurship implies facing challenges on the grounds that entrepreneurs attempts to enhance new items, new techniques for creation and promoting. Self employment, then again, implies either no gamble or very little gamble. However, when the self employed individual beginnings becoming imaginative and does whatever it may take to grow his business, he turns into an entrepreneur. In this way, self employment turns into a take off platform for business.

• Promotion of Individualised Services

Self employment may likewise appear as offering individualized types of assistance like fitting, fix work, apportioning of medications, and so on. Such administrations are useful in giving better customer fulfillment. These can be handily begun and run by people.

• Scope of Creativity

It gives a valuable open door to improvement of imagination and abilities in workmanship and specialties, prompting protection of the social legacy of India. For instance, we can see imaginative thoughts reflected in handiworks, handloom items, and so on.

• Reducing the Problem of Unemployment

Self employment gives chances of beneficial occupation to the people who in any case stay jobless. In this manner it lessens the issue of joblessness.

• A boon to Under-privileged in Respect of Higher Education

Everybody will most likely be unable to seek after advanced education after Secondary or Senior Secondary assessment because of either reason. Such people can begin their profession as self employed in occupations that don't need advanced education.

Characteristics of Successful Entrepreneurs (Entrepreneurial Traits):
Enterprising traits are the normal qualities, capacities and thought designs related with fruitful business visionaries. While certain entrepreneurs brought into the world with these characteristics, others can

foster them

1. A sense of wonder (Curiosity) -

Successful entrepreneurs have a natural curiosity that permits them to seek out new opportunities on a regular basis. Rather than settling for what they think they know, inquisitive entrepreneurs pose difficult questions and pursue new paths.

Entrepreneurship is described as a "process of discovery" in Entrepreneurship Essentials.

Valuable discoveries might easily be overlooked if you don't have the motivation to keep asking questions and challenging the established quo.

2. Experimentation with a Plan -

Curiosity necessitates the use of systematic experimentation. An entrepreneur must conduct tests on each new opportunity to assess whether it is worthwhile to pursue.

If you have a concept for a new product or service that fills a gap in the market, you'll need to make sure clients are willing to pay for it. To accomplish so, you'll need to perform extensive market research and run relevant experiments to confirm your concept and assess its viability.

3. Flexibility (Adaptability) -

The nature of business is constantly evolving. Entrepreneurship is a continuous process in which new difficulties and possibilities arise at regular intervals. It's practically hard to anticipate every eventuality. When unexpected events occur, entrepreneurs must examine the situation and adjust in order to keep their business moving forward.

4. Determination -

An entrepreneur must make difficult decisions and stick to them in order to be successful. As a leader, they're in charge of steering their company's course, which includes everything from funding and strategy to resource allocation.

Having all the answers does not always imply being decisive. If you want to be an entrepreneur, you must have the courage to make difficult decisions and follow through. If the outcome isn't what you expected, the decision to take corrective action is just as critical.

5. Creating a Team -

A good entrepreneur understands his or her own strengths and weaknesses. Rather than allowing their weaknesses to hold them back, they create well-rounded teams that match their strengths.

In many cases, the entrepreneurial team, not an individual, is the driving force behind a venture's success. It's vital to surround yourself with teammates that have complimentary skills and contribute to a similar objective while beginning your own firm.

6. Tolerance for Risk -

Risk is frequently associated with entrepreneurship. While it is true that starting a business requires an entrepreneur to accept risks, they must also take actions to reduce those risks.

Many things might go wrong while starting a new business, but many things can also go right. Entrepreneurs must actively manage the risk-reward connection and position their businesses to "profit from the upside," according to Entrepreneurship Essentials.

Successful entrepreneurs are willing to take some risk in order to gain the benefits of their labours; yet, their risk tolerance is closely linked to their risk mitigation efforts.

7. At Ease With Failure -

Entrepreneurship necessitates a certain level of comfort with failure, in addition to managing risk and making informed judgments.

Nearly 75% of new businesses fail, according to estimates. Failure can be caused by a variety of factors, ranging from a defective company plan to a lack of focus or ambition. Many of these dangers can be avoided, while some are unavoidable.

Successful entrepreneurs are prepared for failure and are at ease with it. Rather of allowing fear to hold them back, they are propelled ahead by the prospect of accomplishment.

8. Perseverance -

While many successful entrepreneurs are aware of the prospect of failure, this does not mean they are easily discouraged. Failures, on the other hand, are viewed as opportunities to learn and progress.

Many theories are proven to be incorrect during the entrepreneurial process, and some ventures fail completely. Part of what makes a good entrepreneur is their desire to learn from their mistakes, ask questions, and persevere until they achieve their goal.

9. Creativity -

Many people believe that entrepreneurship and invention go hand in hand. This is frequently true—some of the most successful firms have taken existing products or services and substantially upgraded them to satisfy market demands.

Some entrepreneurs, but not all, have the ability to innovate. It is, however, a form of strategic thinking that may be developed. You can be well-equipped to detect new ideas and position your enterprise for success by honing your strategic thinking skills.

10. Focus on the Long Run -

Finally, the majority of people associate entrepreneurship with the act of beginning a firm. While the early stages of a venture's development are crucial to its success, the process does not cease once the company is up and running.

"It's easy to establish a business, but hard to create a sustainable and substantial one," according to Entrepreneurship Essentials. Some of history's most significant chances were identified long after a venture had begun."

Entrepreneurship is a long-term undertaking, and to be successful in the long run, entrepreneurs must focus on the process from start to finish.

Different forms of business organization:

The phrase "business organisation" refers to how businesses are organised and how that structure aids them in achieving their objectives. Businesses are generally designed to focus on either making a profit or benefiting society. A for-profit organisation is one that is only focused on making money. A non-profit (or not-for-profit) organisation is one that focuses on advancing the social good through the arts, education, health care, or some other sector and is not commonly referred to as a corporation. .An entity founded for the purpose of carrying on a commercial operation is referred to as a business organisation. The foundations of such an organisation include legal systems that control contract and exchange, property rights, and incorporation.

Sole proprietorship, partnership, corporation, and Limited Liability Company, or LLC, are the four primary types of business entities.

Sole Proprietorship:

A sole proprietorship is a business that is owned and operated by one person. It is the simplest and most frequent type of business ownership. It is a business that is owned and operated only for the profit of the owner. Because the business's survival is totally dependent on the person's decisions, when the owner dies, the business dies with him.

Advantages:

- All profits belong to the owner.

- Proprietorships are subject to relatively minimal regulation.
- When it comes to running the business, owners have complete control.
- There are few requirements for getting started—often only a business licence.

Disadvantages:

- The owner is fully responsible for the company's debts.
- The owner's personal assets are the only source of equity.
- It is difficult to transfer proprietorship ownership.
- There isn't a distinction between personal and business earnings.

Partnership:

There are two categories of these: general and limited. In general, both partners spend their money, property, labour, and other resources in the firm and are equally liable for its debts. In other words, even if you just put a small amount of money into a general partnership, you could be held liable for the entire debt. General partnerships do not require a written agreement; between the two firm owners, partnerships might be implicit or even verbal.

A formal agreement between the partners is required for limited partnerships. They must also file a partnership certificate with the state. Limited partnerships allow partners to minimise their personal liability for corporate debts based on their ownership or investment percentage.

Advantages:

- Shared resources allow the company to raise additional funds.
- Each partner receives a portion of the company's overall profits.
- A proprietorship has a similar level of flexibility and simplicity.
- It is inexpensive to form a legal or informal business partnership.

Disadvantages:

- Each partner is solely accountable for all debts and losses.
- It's difficult to sell a business because it necessitates finding a new partner.
- When one of the partners decides to end the partnership, it ends.

Corporation:

Corporations are regarded legal persons and are considered separate entities for tax reasons. This means, among other things, that a corporation's profits are taxed as "personal income" of the corporation. The income delivered to shareholders as dividends or profits is then taxed as the owners' personal income.

Advantages:

- Limits the owner's liability for debts or losses.
- The corporation owns the profits and losses.
- It is relatively simple to transfer ownership to new proprietors.
- It is not possible to seize personal assets to pay off commercial debts.

Disadvantages:

- Corporate activities are expensive.
- The expense of forming a corporation is high.
- To start a corporate business, you'll need a lot of documentation.
- Corporate income is taxed twice, with limited exceptions.

Limited Liability Corporation (LLC):

An LLC, like a limited partnership, limits shareholders' liability while giving some of the revenue benefits of a partnership. In essence, an LLC combines the benefits of partnerships and corporations, reducing some of the negatives of both.

Advantages:

- Limits the company owners' liability for debts or losses.
- The LLC's revenues are split among the shareholders without being taxed twice.

Disadvantages:

- Certain state regulations restrict ownership.
- Comprehensive and sophisticated agreements are required.
- Due to legal and filing requirements, forming an LLC is expensive.

Type of Firm	Advantages	Disadvantages
Individual Proprietorship	1. Business is simple to set up. 2. Decisionmaking is clear-cut 3. Earnings are taxed only once as personal income.	1. The owner has unlimited liability 2. The owner makes the decisions. 3. Business dies with owner.
Partnership	1. Business is relatively easy to set up. 2. More management skills are available; two heads are better than one. 3. Earnings are taxed only once as the personal income of the partners.	1. There is unlimited liability for the partners. 2. Decisionmaking can be complicated. 3. The company has a limited ability to raise capital. 4. Partnerships can be unstable.
Corporation	1. There is limited liability for owners. 2. A corporation has a separate legal status. It is able to raise large sums of capital through issuing bonds and stock. 3. It has an eternal life or perpetual existence. 4. It is able to recruit professional management and to change bad management due to separation of ownership from management.	1. Corporate income is taxed twice : once as corporate profits, then as personal income (dividends). 2. There are greater possibilities for management disagreements. 3. There is the possibility of conflicting goals between the owners of the corporation (the principals) and management (the agents).

Types of Business Organisations

Entrepreneurship may be defined as identifying change, seeking opportunity, accepting risk and responsibility, inventing, bettering resource utilisation, producing new value that is significant to customers, and repeating the process.

The Public Sector

The Public Sector is made up of firms that are owned and controlled by a country's government. The central or state governments have either entire or partial ownership and management of these organizations. However, it still owns the bulk of the company and makes all of the company's decisions. Government agencies, state-owned companies, municipalities, local government authorities, and other public service institutions are among these organizations. Some may be non-profit organizations, while others may also engage in commercial activity. Its main goal is to provide goods and services to the general public at lower prices than private businesses. Its fundamental goal is to ensure the general wellbeing of a country's citizens.

The Private Sector

Individuals or corporate entities own, control, and manage private-sector firms. It could be a small, medium, or even a large organization. These are founded to profit from their operations and can raise funds from people, groups, and the general public. Sole proprietorships, partnerships, cooperative societies, businesses, and multinational corporations are all examples of private sector entities. To survive in the long run, they also concentrate on meeting the demands of their clients. Almost every industry in India has been opened to the private sector since the adoption of the New Economic Policy by the Indian government in 1991. As a result, the size of the economy has exploded.

What is the definition of a private-sector enterprise?

A component of the national economy is referred to as the private sector. A private collection of persons, or possibly a single corporation, owns and controls these. There are numerous companies in this industry, which are classified according to their size and functional capabilities. It comprises both small and major businesses. They can be privately held or publicly traded. In most cases, a private enterprise is founded by forming a new corporation. Existing public-sector enterprises, on the other hand, may be privatized. Typically, these businesses are conducted with a single goal in mind: to make the most money possible. Building a brand reputation is typically used to promote this strategy. These businesses must adhere to government guidelines and rules. These, however, are not under the supervision of the government.

In general, private businesses provide the most jobs in a given economy. They are primarily concerned with an employee's performance in order to ensure his or her job security. The following is a list of some of the most well-known private sector examples in a given economy.

What is the definition of a public-sector company?

The fact that they are owned, controlled, and managed by government organizations is the single distinguishing trait that students must grasp when learning about the public sector. A government body can have whole or partial ownership, control, and administration of a property. Importantly, these businesses are normally within the jurisdiction of specific ministries and are functionally managed by them. Parliamentary actions only set up a small number of public sector firms. Both their operation and control are defined by these acts. A public enterprise primarily serves the general public by delivering lower-cost goods and services. It encompasses federal, state, and municipal government institutions. Depending on the level of government supervision, this industry can be split into two categories.

CHAPTER II

ENTREPRENEURIAL SUPPORT SYSTEM: SOURCES OF INFORMATION, POLICIES AND SCHEMES FOR PROMOTION OF MSME, MARKET SURVEY&OPPORTUNITY IDENTIFICATION

INTRODUCTION

Entrepreneurial support systems help the entire community. By boosting collaboration, improving efficiency, and increasing effectiveness, these systems have a revolutionary impact on economic development. Increased employment generation, new business development, existing business growth, and enhanced overall quality of life are some of the other results. Entrepreneurial communities aim to support and develop existing entrepreneurs as well as attract new ones.

The following are the components of an entrepreneurial support system:

1. Opportunities for networking and mentoring
2. Local knowledge base and educational initiatives
3. Financial and capital resources
4. Encouragement and assistance for entrepreneurial endeavors
5. Public policy that fosters new ventures and innovation

Ways to Build an Entrepreneurial Support System

Starting and running a new business can be isolating and frightening. During a crisis, there is no longer a boss to manage things. No more clocking out at 5 p.m. and abandoning the job. Entrepreneurship means that your work is your life—and when things get too much to handle, having an entrepreneurial support system is critical to the success of your business.

Internal, external, or a combination of the two can serve as your support system. My business partners and I agree on the big things, like setting goals, working hard, and supporting each other in times of crisis. However, when it comes to time management or dealing with stress, we sometimes need to look beyond our immediate circle.

Don't put off establishing a support system until a crisis occurs. You need an entrepreneurial support system in place to help you quickly resolve your issue and move on. Here are some suggestions for who should be on your team and where you can get help.

1. **Other business owners are an obvious entrepreneurial support system.**

It's always a good idea to solicit opinions and advice from other business owners, even if they're not in your industry. Make time to connect over coffee, lunch, or even the phone if distance or time constraints exist. I recently met with several of my former employees who are now entrepreneurs, which has resulted in new business. My go-to IT person is a former employee of mine.

2. Mentors are also beneficial.

"People are afraid to ask for help because they don't like feeling vulnerable," a psychologist friend of mine once told me. Asking for help from others can often feel like we're giving up some control over our own businesses. That is especially difficult for entrepreneurs to do, but the value of having mentors is worth feeling vulnerable for a moment.

3. Other industry professionals

According to a Barlow Research study conducted last year, when business owners were asked who they seek advice from, the overwhelming response was their accountants.

4. Online communities are widely available.

You've probably discovered that you can find almost anything online, including a community of like-minded entrepreneurs seeking (and willing to provide) advice and support. There are hundreds of online communities you can join and benefit from (such as American Express OPEN). For online communities specific to your market, contact your industry trade association.

Many times, entrepreneurship can appear to be a lonely pursuit. You will be better prepared to deal with the inevitable highs and lows of business ownership if you create a support system.

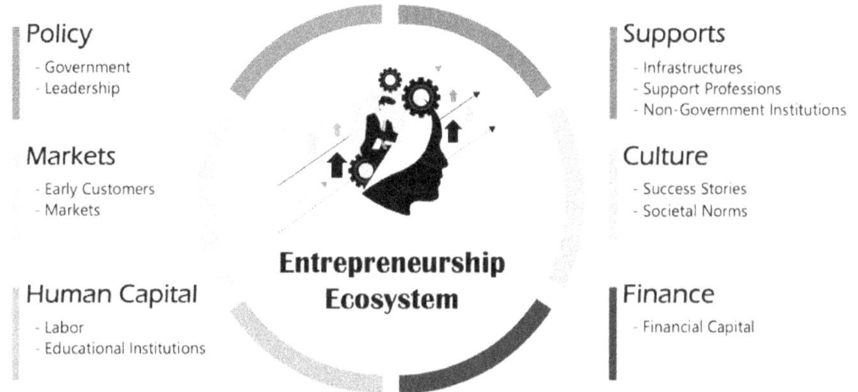

Source: The World Economic Forum

The state and federal governments have established a variety of specialized agencies to promote entrepreneur growth, including:

1. Service Institutes for Small Businesses (SISI)

2. Small Business Development Organizations (SBDOs) (SIDO)

3. National Small Business Administration

4. Small Industries Extension Training Institute (SIETI) is a training institute for small businesses.

5. India's Entrepreneurship Development Institute

6. Rural Management and Administration Institute

7. The National Institute for Entrepreneurship and Small Business Development is a non-profit organization that promotes entrepreneurship and small business development (NIESBUD)

8. Young Entrepreneurs' National Alliance (NAYA)

9. Maharashtra Centre for Entrepreneurship Development (Maharashtra Centre for Entrepreneurship Development) (MCED)

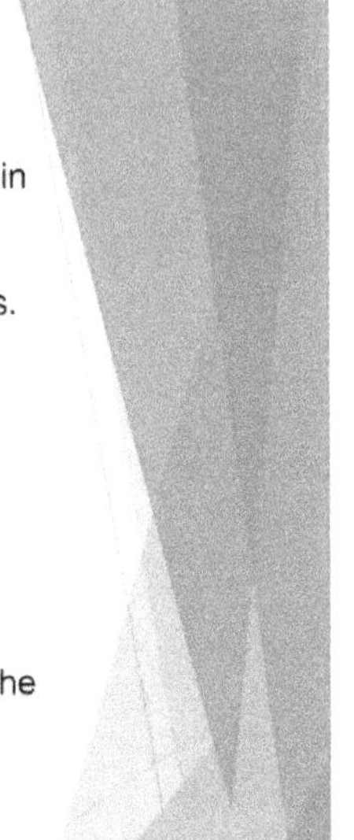

SOURCE: slideplayer.com

To develop their startup ideas into profitable businesses, entrepreneurs require a strong support and advisory system. Supporting entrepreneurship is critical to our lives' growth and betterment. Innovations and effective solutions to current challenges are required in today's world society. Entrepreneurs' bright and ambitious minds are to turn their game-changing ideas into profitable organizations with a mission, guided by their vision. We promote innovation by supporting entrepreneurs.

THE ROLE OF GOVERNMENT IN SUPPORTING ENTREPRENEURSHIP

SMEs have strategic importance for each national economy due a wide range of reasons such as:

• Simpler way to create new job positions,

• Increasing GDP and

• Rising standard of population

Therefore, government are supporting entrepreneurship and encouraging and supporting people who dare to start their own business. Every surviving and successful business means new jobs and growth of GDP

• Therefore, Council of Ministers and entity governments provide full coordination of activities through numerous governmental institutions (like chambers of commerce, employment bureaus, etc.) and NGOs dealing with entrepreneurship and SMEs

• Governments create different types of support institutions:

To provide information on regulations, standards, taxation, customs duties, marketing issues;

To advise on business planning, marketing and accountancy, quality control and assurance to create incubator units providing the space and infrastructure for business beginners and innovative companies, and helping them to solve technological problems, and to search for know how and promote innovation; and to help in looking for partners in order to stimulate entrepreneurship and improve the husness environment for small enterprise.

POLICIES AND SCHEMES FOR PROMOTION OF MSME IMPLEMENTED BY STATE GOVERNMENTS

All the State Governments provide technical and other support services to small units through their Directorates of Industries, and District Industries Centers. The details of the scheme vary from state to state, the following are the common support.

Development and management of industrial estates

- Suspension/deferment of Sales Tax
- Power subsidies
- Capital investment subsidies for new units set up in a particular district
- Seed Capital/ Margin Money Assistance Scheme
- Priority in allotment of power connection, water connection.

Government of India runs a scheme for giving National Awards to micro, small and medium scale entrepreneurs providing quality products in 11 selected industry groups of consumer interest. The

winners are given trophy, certificate and a cash price of R. 25000/- each. Through framing and implementing suitable policies and promotional schemes, government play supportive role in developing entrepreneurs.

SOURCES OF INFORMATION

1. The library is an important information source. There are a range of materials available from government entities that you could find useful. Some colleges and institutions have reference libraries with public access to the circulating section.

In addition, several larger companies and research institutes maintain libraries with sections dedicated to specific topics. Libraries are a great source of information that can help you run a small business.

Books, journals, reports, and newspapers may include knowledge that can support in the solution of some business challenges.

2. The Internet may be used to conduct research and uncover valuable facts and information. Google, Bing, Ask, and others are examples of these search engines. E-mail can also be used to communicate with information providers who have websites on the internet.

3. Purchasing trade papers and magazines on a regular basis. Entrepreneurs should set aside time to read articles, particularly in order to keep up with new business trends and advancements.

It's a good idea to keep a file of relevant articles for future use.

4. Commercial when comparing a company to others in its industry, data is quite useful. Data on stock turnover, cash discounts, percentage mark-up, and other ratios is accessible from trade associations or government agencies.

5. Membership-based organizations can undertake research, organize education and training programmers, implement new technologies, respond to members' inquiries and concerns, and disseminate information through newsletters, magazines, and special reports, among other services.

MAN is an example of a membership-based organization (Manufacturers Association of Nigeria)

6. Entrepreneurs can use training programmers to create formal plans for enhancing their managerial skills and abilities. Many institutions, agencies, and associations create training courses and adult education programmers.

Entrepreneurs should be aware of these opportunities for personal development and take advantage of them.

7. Employees. People who work for a company might provide solutions to specific business difficulties. Entrepreneurs may, for example, seek employee input and support on merchandise display or customer attitudes. Employees are in an excellent position to provide useful recommendations if they believe their ideas and opinions are valued.

Customers can also provide extremely detailed information about the products and services they purchase. Customers should be polled for their thoughts because they are a valuable source of information regarding a company's relative strengths and faults.

8. Other business owners. Most firms have similar issues, and their owners are often willing to talk about them with one another.

The competitive nature of the business may sometimes prevent this open discussion, but if the businesses are unconnected and do not compete for the same clients, entrepreneurs may be prepared to share ideas about how to solve a common problem. All business owners can profit from this contact and improve their operations in this way.

Basis	Primary Source of Information	Secondary Source of Information	Tertiary Source of Information
Meaning	Primary sources are original materials collected from the time period involved and have not been filtered through interpretation or valuation. They present original thinking, report a discovery, or share new information.	It refers to all those information collected through original information, and after that further modified, selected or rearranged for a specific purpose or objectives. It is also called as an interpretations and evaluations of primary sources.	It refers to all those information which is a distillation and collection of primary and secondary sources.
Information	The data is collected by the investigator himself/herself, for the first time. They present first hand accounts and information relevant to an event.	One that was created by someone who did not have first hand experience or did not participate in the events/situations being researched.	It may be second hand or third hand and not considered to be acceptable material on which to base academic research are usually not credited to a particular author.
Description	The information is described its original form, not interpreted, condensed or valuated any other people.	It describes, analyse, interpret, evaluate, comment on and discuss the evidence given by primary sources.	Are intended only to describe and provide an overview of what the topic includes, its basic terminology, and often references for further reading.

SOURCE : learncbse. In

MARKET SURVEY

A market survey entails conducting research and analyzing the market for a specific product or service, as well as looking into customer preferences. Market surveys are tools for gathering direct input from a target audience in order to better understand their traits, expectations, and needs.

Most marketing managers rely on market surveys to gather data that will help them kick start their market research. In addition, the information gathered from these surveys can help with product marketing and feature enhancement.

Market surveys gather information about a target market, such as pricing patterns, customer needs, competitor analyses, and other relevant information.

A market survey is an organized and in-depth method that covers all of the research tasks associated with carefully obtaining information from sources for the first time.

Purpose of Market Survey

1. **Gain crucial customer feedback:** The market survey's main goal is to provide marketing and business managers with a platform to gather critical information about their customers so that existing customers can be kept and new ones can be recruited.
2. **Recognize client preferences for acquiring products:** Details include whether customers are willing to spend a specific amount of money on their products/services, customer propensity levels toward new features or products, what they think about competitor products, and so on.
3. **Enhance existing products and services:** A market survey can be used to improve existing products, examine customer satisfaction levels, and obtain information about their market perceptions, as well as to create a buyer persona utilizing data from an existing clientele database.
4. **Make well-informed company judgments:** Market survey data is useful for making big changes in the firm, reducing the amount of risk associated in making critical business decisions.

The following is an example of how to conduct a survey in the typical way:

The first step is to plan the survey.

Fieldwork is the second step.

Step third is Data analysis and interpretation

Making a report is the fourth step.

There are two kinds of market research studies:

The census (a) and the sample (b)

The following are the values of a market surveyor:

(a) The fairness with which a survey is conducted.

(b) The survey was conducted with a selfless motive.

(c) Appropriate analysis in order to represent the proper outcome.

(d) Creating a one-of-a-kind questionnaire to elicit the correct response from customers.

OPPORTUNITY IDENTIFICATION

When entrepreneurs look for opportunities in existing markets, they find them. This implies they keep track of technological, economic, and social developments. Opportunities are recognized through a cognitive process. It is based on people's capacity to recognize patterns and connect the dots.

Entrepreneurs create possibilities when they collaborate with others to bounce ideas back and forth, and each time the consumer needs and how they will be addressed grow more explicit. The process of creating possibilities is a social one. It is based on the ability of entrepreneurs to communicate with one another.

Process of Identifying Business Opportunities

It's crucial to understand how entrepreneurs identify and select new company opportunities that have the best potential of succeeding. The most important aspect of any business endeavors, as seen in the majority of successful businesses, is addressing an unmet market demand. Customers are continuously looking for things that offer value to their lives. They purchase things that are only required to solve a certain problem.

Most entrepreneurs who are looking for new business ideas think about three main challenges. The most important is the potential financial worth. He or she initially assesses whether the venture has the potential to be profitable. The second factor is the venture's infancy. He or she will favor products, services, or technologies that have never been seen in that setting before. The third consideration is if their product is morally or legally acceptable in that context. He then evaluates

- Whether his final business choice concept fills a gap in the market.
- Whether he has the resources and expertise to carry out this business idea.
- Its market is readily available, and it sells at a profit.
- The new business idea will be able to compete competitively with similar competitors and their markets.
- Whether or not this company market is expanding, and how one should prepare to enter it.

The Process of Identifying Opportunities in Stages

The entrepreneur's history, business impact, and the overall business climate are the three key components that go into identifying an opportunity. The five phases of opportunity identification lead to 'recognition.' The five stages are explored in reference to the process of identifying opportunities.

a. preparation b. incubation c. insight d. evaluation and e. elaboration

OPPORTUNITY IDENTIFICATION PROCESS

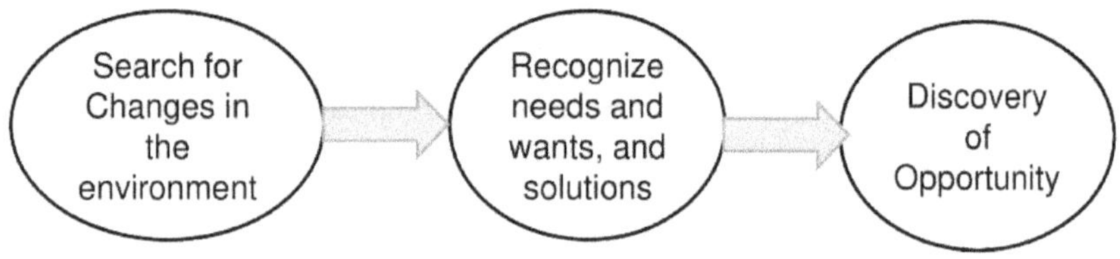

Source: Startup amity

- **Preparation**

The information and experience gained just prior to the opportunity discovery process is referred to as the preparation stage. These skills and experiences are rarely obtained consciously. Preparation, on the other hand, is frequently an intentional endeavor to broaden capability in a certain area and become sensitive to issues in a particular field of interest. The background of the business, the products or services, or technological knowledge must have heavily influenced the core ideas of the successful endeavor in a well-organized setting. However, new ideas and expertise emerging from individuals within the firm that will eventually result in a new business cannot be ruled out.

- **Incubation**

The incubation stage of the opportunity identification process entails a businessman or his team considering a notion or a specific problem that has not been subjected to conscious or formal study. It's usually not done intentionally, and as a result, it's more often than not an instinctual and unempirical method to weighing multiple viable options.

- **Insight**

The insight stage happens when a basic answer is recognized abruptly and unexpectedly. It's a specific point in time that continues to recurring throughout the opportunity identification process. Insights have been discovered to be broad channels for the discovery of startup enterprises, and they can occasionally reveal more knowledge for the development of an existing discovery method. In the context of a commercial enterprise, insight usually entails the sudden realization of a business opportunity, the solution to a well-considered dilemma, and the acquisition of a concept via social networks and partners.

- **Evaluation**

The evaluation stage entails determining whether the recognized and developed ideas are practical, whether the businessman has the necessary skills to implement the ideas, and whether the idea is sufficiently original for potential customers. It may include a complete feasibility examination of the concepts using a variety of research instruments as well as feedback from key business contacts. The prospect and viability of new insight ideas must also be investigated, as the spirit of entrepreneurship is to create satisfactory and sensible earnings.

- **Elaboration**

Elaboration is the step in which the opportunity/ideas are exposed to external analysis through the laborious and time–consuming process of option selection, choice decision, and resource arrangement. It is normally in search of all legalities that could build trust and ensure the business's viability. Elaboration also minimizes uncertainty by offering specific planning activities after the viability of the evaluation has been confirmed. This will eventually disclose the portions of the notion that require additional examination and attention.

Although aspiring entrepreneurs can generate ideas all day, not every idea is viable. To determine whether a concept is worthwhile to pursue, we must first determine whether it can be transformed into a business opportunity. The entrepreneurial opportunity is the point at which recognised consumer demand meets the practicality of delivering the requested product or service. Several conditions must be met in order to progress from an idea to an opportunity in the field of entrepreneurship. It all starts with cultivating the right mindset—one in which the aspiring entrepreneur sharpens their senses to consumer needs and wants and conducts research to determine whether the concept has the potential to become a profitable new venture.

Reading as much as you can, especially about new technological advances, even outside of your line of work, is a fantastic beginning to start your entrepreneurial journey. Remember that when new technologies arise, we often have no idea what their commercial potential is. Microwave technology, for example, was first used in radars to track Navy submarines. The microwave, however, was invented thanks to an inquisitive man named Percy Spencer and the unintentional melting of a peanut bar in his pocket while toying with the technology one day. It would take decades for it to be created at a cost that the general public could pay.

CHAPTER III

ELEMENTS OF MANAGEMEN: PRINCIPLES OF MANAGEMENT, MANAGERIAL FUNCTIONS&VALUE OF HUMAN RELATIONS IN MANAGEMENT

Introduction:

What exactly is management?

Management is the process of organising and planning a company's resources and activities in order to achieve specific goals in the most effective and efficient way possible. In management, efficiency refers to the completion of tasks correctly and at the lowest possible cost. Management effectiveness is defined as the completion of tasks within specific time frames to produce tangible results.Management (or managing) is the process of overseeing the operations of a company, a non-profit organisation, or a government agency. It's the art and science of managing a company's resources.

Management entails developing an organization's strategy and organising the efforts of its employees (or volunteers) to achieve its goals through the use of available resources such as financial, natural, technological, and human resources. "Run the business" and "Change the business" are two management concepts that differentiate between continuing to provide goods or services and adapting goods or services to changing customer needs - see trend. The term "management" can also refer to the people in charge of the operations of an organization—managers.

Definitions:

Views on the definition and scope of management include –

- **Henri Fayol** (1841–1925) stated: "to manage is to forecast and to plan, to organise, to command, to co-ordinate and to control."
- **Fredmund Malik** (1944–) defines management as "the transformation of resources into utility".

- Management is included as one of the factors of production – along with machines, materials and money.
- **Ghislain Deslandes** defines management as "a vulnerable force, under pressure to achieve results and endowed with the triple power of constraint, imitation and imagination, operating on subjective, interpersonal, institutional and environmental levels".
- **Peter Drucker** (1909–2005) saw the basic task of management as twofold: marketing and innovation. Nevertheless, innovation is also linked to marketing (product innovation is a central strategic marketing issue). Drucker identifies marketing as a key essence for business success, but management and marketing are generally understood as two different branches of business administration knowledge

Principles of management:

The History of 14 Management Principles Have a Long -

Henry Fayol is regarded as the father of modern management theory. During the height of the French Industrial Revolution, he worked as an engineer for the Compagnie de Commentry-Fourchambault-Decazeville mining firm, eventually rising to the position of manager. Under his leadership, the struggling company thrived.

In 1916, he published "Administration Industrielle et Générale," a book about his experiences managing a workforce. This laid the foundation for administrative philosophy as well as the 14 Management Principles. By emphasising administrative rather than technical skills, these concepts became one of the earliest examples of treating management as a legitimate profession.

Principles of Management-Nature and types

Principles of management describe the general guidelines for better decisions of the managers. These are applied with creativity and are flexible in nature.

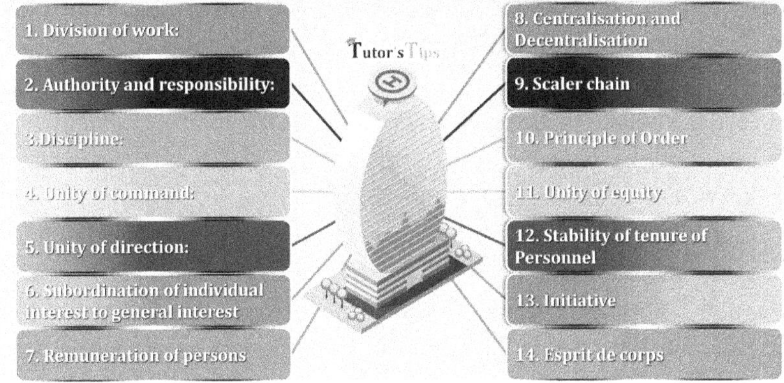

Source: Management Study HQ

Fayol The 14 Management Principles of Henry -

The 14 management principles of Henry Fayol look at an organisation from the top down to assist managers get the most out of employees and run the firm smoothly. Let's take a closer look at them and figure out what they mean.

1. Division of work -

The first management principle is founded on the idea that by assigning a specific task to an employee, they will become more efficient and skilled at it. This is in contrast to a multi-tasking culture, in which one employee is given a large number of duties to complete at the same time. Examine each employee's present skill sets and assign them a task that they can master in order to effectively implement this approach. In the long run, this will help them become more productive, skilled, and efficient.

2. Authority -

This principle emphasises that a manager must have the appropriate authority to ensure that his or her staff follow his or her orders. If managers lacked authority, they would be unable to do any tasks. This power, however, should be accompanied with accountability. There should be a balance between authority and accountability, according to Henri Fayol.

Employees will become upset if there is more authority than duty. The manager will be irritated if there is more responsibility than authority.

3. Discipline -

This notion asserts that any organization's success depends on its ability to maintain discipline. Managers must create a culture of mutual respect in order to have disciplined employees. A set of organisational norms, principles, and structures should be in place and followed by everyone. In any company, breaking regulations or laziness should not be tolerated. In order to accomplish this, good supervision and impartial judgement are required.

4. Unity of command -

This principle states that in the organisation, there should be a clear chain of command. Employees should be clear about who's orders they should obey. Only one boss should issue commands to an employee, according to Fayol. When an employee reports to two or more bosses, authority, discipline, and consistency are jeopardised. Furthermore, this will result in a management structure breakdown and employee burnout.

5. Unity of direction -

This principle asserts that work should be organised such that people work together toward a common goal, following a single plan, and reporting to a single management. If you have a variety of marketing tasks, such as advertising, budgeting, and sales promotion, for example, you should have one manager that oversees all of them. Different sub-managers can be assigned to different duties, but they should all work toward a shared goal under the supervision of a single primary person in control of everything.

6. Collective interest over individual interest -

This principle emphasises that the team's overall interests should take precedence above individual interests. Individual interests should not be allowed to sabotage the organization's goals. The group will implode if someone goes renegade.

7. Remuneration -

Employees should be paid a fair compensation for the work they do, according to this notion. Any company that underpays its employees will have a hard time motivating and retaining good employees. Financial and non-financial incentives should be included in this remuneration. In order to motivate staff, there should also be a mechanism in place to recognise good performance.

8. Centralization -

The consolidation of power in the hands of the authority and the use of a top-down management method are both examples of centralization. This authority is distributed to all levels of management in decentralisation. No organisation can be entirely centralised or decentralised in today's world. People at the bottom have no authority over their obligations due to complete centralization. Similarly, complete decentralisation implies that the organisation will be controlled by no higher authority. To use it successfully today, a balance of centralization and decentralisation is required. The degree to which this equilibrium is accomplished varies from one organisation to the next.

9. Scalar Chain -

A clear chain of communication between employees and their superiors is referred to as a scalar chain. Employees should be aware of their position in the organization's hierarchy and who to contact in a chain of command. To put this into practise in the workplace, Fayol recommends drawing up an organisational chart so that employees can understand the structure clearly.

10. Order -

This idea states that resources (manpower, money, materials, etc.) should be placed in the appropriate location at the right time in an organised manner. This guarantees that resources are used properly and in a systematic manner. Misuse and disorder in the organisation will result if any of these resources are misplaced.

11. Equity -

Kindness and justice are combined in equity. This idea emphasises that managers should treat their subordinates with kindness and justice. Employees become more loyal and dedicated to the company they work for as a result of this.

12. Stability of Tenure of Personnel –

According to this theory, a business should strive to reduce personnel turnover while increasing efficiency. It is unrealistic to expect a new employee to quickly adapt to an organization's culture. To become efficient, they must be given ample time to settle into their employment. Job security should be provided to both existing and new employees, as insecurity can lead to inefficiency. Because it costs time and money to educate new employees, there should be a clear and effective system for dealing with vacancies when they emerge.

13. Initiative -

According to this notion, all employees should be encouraged to take initiative. Employees are driven and appreciated when they have a say in how they accomplish their jobs. Organizations should pay attention to their employees' problems and encourage them to develop and implement improvement strategies.

14. Esprit de corps -

The term "esprit de corps" refers to a sense of belonging to a group. This principle argues that management should endeavour to foster staff unity, morale, and cooperation. The organization's team spirit is a huge source of strength. Employees that are happy and motivated are more likely to be productive and efficient.

That was all about principles of management.

What Is the Importance of the 14 Principles of Management?

Henri Fayol was one of the first to draw attention to the distinction between technical and managerial abilities. He emphasised that "manager" is a profession in and of itself, requiring study, teaching, and development. Consider a team with the highest technical talents in the world but no established management procedures. Skills without direction are bound to yield ineffective results.

You don't have to be a good manager to have good technical skills. For planning, forecasting, decision-making, process management, organisation management, coordination, and control, you'll also require a variety of non-technical abilities. All of these skills are taught in the 14 management principles to help managers understand how to run a business efficiently.

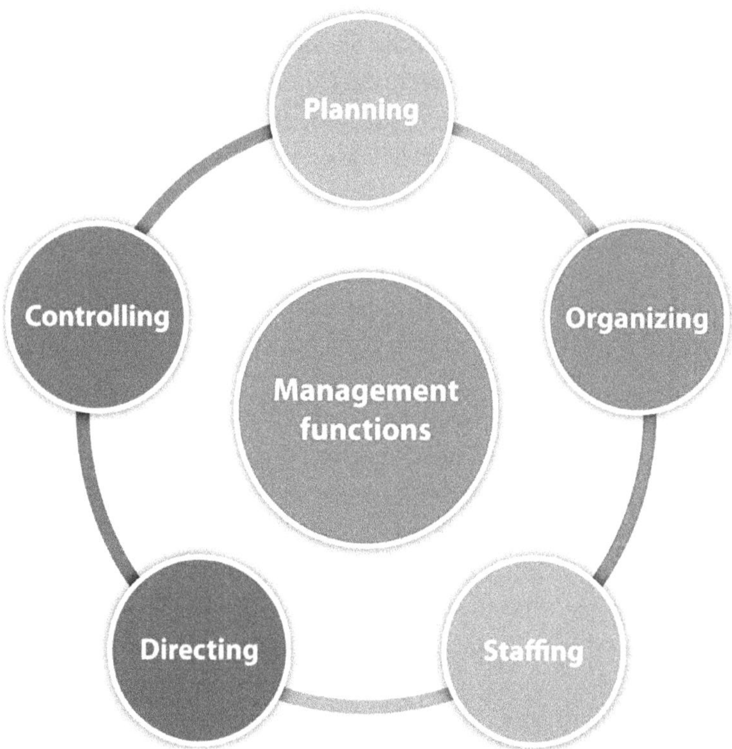

Source – university of Westminster

Managerial functions:

Understanding the functions will help managers focus efforts on activities that gain results. Summarizing the five functions of great management.

1. Planning: In a management capacity, consider of planning as the process of selecting acceptable goals and activities to pursue, then determining what strategies to apply, what actions to take, and what resources are required to attain the goals. It is the most fundamental management role. It is concerned with planning a future course of action and determining the best appropriate path of action for achieving pre-determined objectives.

According to KOONTZ, "Planning is deciding in advance - what to do, when to do & how to do. It bridges the gap from where we are & where we want to be". A strategy is a set of actions that will be taken in the future. It's a problem-solving and decision-making activity.

Planning entails deciding on a path of action to attain a set of objectives. As a result, planning is a methodical consideration of strategies and means for achieving predetermined objectives. Planning is required to ensure that human and non-human resources are properly utilised. It is widespread, it is an intellectual activity, and it aids in the avoidance of ambiguity, uncertainty, dangers, and waste, among other things.

IMPORTANCE OF PLANNING

- **Planning increases efficiency** – Planning makes optimum utilization of all available resources. It helps to reduce wastage and avoids duplication of work.

- **Planning reduces business-related risks** - Planning helps to forecast the business–related risk and also helps to take necessary precautions to avoid these risks and prepare for future uncertainties

- **Planning provides direction** – Direction means to give proper information, accurate instructions and guidance to the subordinates. Planning tells us what to do, how to do and when to do. It helps the organization to achieve its goals through systematic coordination of the employees.

- **Planning encourages creativity and innovation**- Planning helps managers to express their creativity and innovation. It brings satisfaction to the managers and eventually success to the organization.

- **Planning helps in motivation**- A good plan provides various financial and non-financial incentives to both managers and employees. These incentives motivate them to work hard and achieve the objectives of the organizaition.

- **Planning helps in decision making** – A manager makes many different plans. Then they evaluate every course of action and choose the best strategy. So, decision-making is facilitated by planning.

- **Planning helps to achieve objectives**- Without Planning each and every activity will be based on trial and error which will give rise to confusion Every organization has certain targets. Planning helps an organization to achieve their aims by avoiding overlapping, confusion and misunderstanding.

2. **Organizing:** This process of forming worker relationships helps employees to collaborate in order to attain organisational objectives.

It is the process of bringing physical, financial, and human resources together and building effective relationships between them in order to achieve organisational goals.

"To organise a business is to provide it with everything useful for its functioning, such as raw material, tools, capital, and personnel," says Henry Fayol. Organizing a company entails identifying and allocating human and non-human resources to the organisational structure.

IMPORTANCE OF ORGANISING

- **It facilitates efficient management** - Organising is necessary for the performance of other functions of management. The poor organisation may result in duplication of work and efforts.
- **It facilitates coordination and communication** - Organisation creates a clear-cut relationship between the departments and helps in laying down balanced emphasis on various activities. It also provides channels of communication and coordination of activities of different departments.
- **It facilitates growth and diversification**- Sound organization helps in the growth and expansion of the enterprise by facilitating its efficient management. It also increases the capacity of the enterprise to undertake more activities.
- **It ensures optimum use of resources** - Organising leads to the optimum use of all material, financial and human resources. It matches the jobs with the individuals and vice versa and ensures that job position is clearly defined. It minimizes confusion and wastage of resources.
- **It provides for optimum use of technological innovations** - Sound organisation structure is not rigid. It is flexible and provides adequate scope for adoption of new technology.
- **It facilitates specialization** - Organising provides a great scope for bringing specialization in every department of an enterprise through proper allocation of jobs among the employees. Organising thus can be understood in two ways:

3. Staffing: Recruiting and selecting individuals for company employment is referred to as staffing (within teams and departments).

It is the task of staffing and maintaining the organization's structure. Staffing has become more important in recent years as a result of technological advancements, increased corporate scale, and the complexity of human behaviour, among other factors.

Staffing's major goal is to match the correct person to the right task, i.e. square pegs in square holes and round pegs in round holes. "Managerial function of staffing" is "manning the organisation structure through proper and effective selection, assessment, and development of employees to fit the responsibilities designed in the structure," according to Kootz and O'Donell. Staffing entails:

IMPORTANCE OF STAFFING

- **Helps in finding efficient worker**- Staffing helps in discovering talented and competent workers and develops them to work more efficiently for achievement of organizational goals.

- **Helps in increased Productivity** – Staffing ensures greater production by putting right man at the right job. It helps in improved organisational productivity through proper selection according to requirement

- **Maintains Harmony**- Staffing maintains harmony in the organisation. Through proper staffing, individuals are not just recruited and selected but their performance is regularly appraised and promotions are done. This gives everyone an equal opportunity for getting better compensation which finally results in peace and harmony.

- **Helps in morale boosting**- Job satisfaction keeps the morale high of the employees. Through training and development programmers their efficiency improves and they feel assured of their career advancement

- **Helps in Optimum utilization of human resources**- Staffing helps in proper utilization of the available personnel. Manpower forecasting provides a basis for recruitment, transfer and training of employees. Shortage or surplus of manpower will be revealed by proper manpower planning.

4. Leading (Directing): Using vision, influence, persuasion, and strong communication skills, this duty entails defining a vision, energising staff, inspiring and motivating individuals. It is the task of staffing and maintaining the organization's structure. Staffing has become more important in recent years as a result of technological advancements, increased corporate scale, and the complexity of human behaviour, among other factors. It is the element of the managerial role that enables organisational techniques to function effectively in order to achieve organisational goals. Because planning, organisation, and staffing are merely preparations for completing the work, it is considered the enterprise's life-spark that sets the action of people in motion. The inert-personnel part of management that deals directly with influencing, leading, monitoring, and inspiring subordinates to achieve organisational goals is called direction. The elements of direction are as follows:

- Supervision - The term "supervision" refers to supervisors overseeing the work of subordinates. It is the act of keeping an eye on and directing work and workers.
- Motivation - It is defined as inspiring, stimulating, or urging subordinates to work with passion. For this reason, positive, negative, monetary, and non-monetary incentives may be used.
- Leadership - It is a process by which a manager directs and influences subordinates' work in a desired direction.
- Communication - The process of sharing knowledge, experience, opinion, and so on from one person to another is known as communication. It's a link between two worlds.

IMPORTANCE OF DIRECTING

- **Initiates action**: Direction initiates action that motivates people to convert the resources into productive outputs. It gives substance to managerial function of planning, organising, staffing and controlling. People learn to manage the resources in the most effective way that results in their optimum utilization.
- **Creates a Sound work environment**: If direction are issued in consultation with employees, it creates an environment of understanding where people work to their maximum potential, willingly and enthusiastically to contribute towards organizational goals.
- **Develops managers**: Managers who are personally motivated to work can also direct others to work. Managers develop their skills and competence. Motivation, leadership and communication help in bringing people together. This is beneficial for both the employees and organisation. Direction, thus, prepares future managers.
- **Behavioral satisfaction**: Since direction involves human behavior and psychology, employees feel behaviorally satisfied and personally inspired to achieve organizational goals.

- **Increase in productivity**: Personally satisfied employees contribute towards output and efficiency of the organisation. Direction gets maximum out of subordinates by exploiting their potential and increasing their capabilities to work.
- **Achieves coordination**: Directing aims at continuous supervision of activities. It achieves coordination by ensuring that people work towards planned activities in a coordinated manner. It integrates the action of employees that increase their understanding of mutual interdependence and their collective effort to achieve the organisational goals.
- **Facilitates control**: Coordination brings actual performance in conformity with planned performance. The controlling function is, thus, facilitated through effective direction.
- **Facilitates change**: Direction helps in introducing change in the organization structure and adapting the organization structure to external environment. People are not easily receptive to changes. Direction helps in changing attitude of people in a positive way.
- **Facilitates growth**: Organisation open to change is responsive to growth. Direction harmonizes physical, financial and human resources, balances various parts of the organization and creates commitment amongst people to raise their standards of performance.

5. Controlling: Evaluate your progress toward your objectives, improve your performance, and take action. Set up procedures to assist you in establishing standards so that you can measure, compare, and make judgments.

It6 entails comparing accomplishments to standards and, if necessary, correcting deviations in order to ensure that corporate objectives are met. The goal of regulating is to ensure that everything happens according to the rules. An effective control system aids in the prediction of deviations before they occur.

"Controlling," according to Theo Haimann, "is the process of determining whether or not sufficient progress toward the aims and goals is being made and, if required, acting to correct any divergence.

"Controlling is the measurement and correction of subordinates' performance activities in order to ensure that the enterprise objectives and plans desired to achieve them are being fulfilled," according to Koontz and O'Donell. As a result, controlling entails the following steps:

- Establishment of standard performance.
- Measurement of actual performance.
- Comparison of actual performance with the standards and finding out deviation if any.
- Corrective action.

IMPORTANCE OF CONTROLLING

- **Basis of future action** - Control provides the basis for future actions. It will reduce the chances of mistakes being repeated in future by suggesting preventive steps.
- **Facilitates decision making**- The process of control is complete only when corrective measures have been taken. This requires taking a right decision as to what type of follow up action is to be taken.
- **Facilitates discipline and order** – The existence of control system has a positive impact on the behavior of the employees. They are cautious while performing their duties as they know they are being observed by their superiors.
- **Facilitates Coordination** - Control helps in Coordination of the activities of various departments of the enterprise. It provides them unity of direction.
- **Facilitates motivation** – A control system is most effective when it motivates people to high performance. Since most people respond to a challenge, successfully meeting a tough standard may provide a greater sense of accomplishment.
- **Effective plan Implementation** - Controlling and planning are interdependent. Control is the only means to ensure that the plans are being implemented control points out short comings of not only planning but also other functions of management. Comparison can be done through various Performance report, Personal Observation.

6. Coordination

The management of a modern enterprise is based on the principle of specialization or division of labour. Jobs are broken down into single repetitive tasks and are entrusted to individual either working in the same department or in different departments. To attain the desired results with so much diversification, coordination becomes necessary. So, Coordination is the management of interdependence in work situations. Coordination leads to blending the activities of different individuals and group of individuals for the achievement of certain objectives. According to Henri Fayol "Coordination harmonizes synchronizes and unifies individual efforts for better action and for the achievement of the business objectives."

IMPORTANCE OF COORDINATION

- **Division of labour** – When managers divide work into specialized function or departments, they at the same time create a need for the coordination for these activities. Greater, the division of labour, greater the need for the coordination.
- **Growth in size** - With the growth in size of an enterprise and large employment of people, the task of integrating the activities becomes more complicated. To achieve the desired results, it is important to harmonise individual goals with organisation goals through coordination.
- **Interdependence of units** - The need for coordination in an organisation also arises because of the interdependence of various units. Greater the interdependence of the units, the greater the need for coordination. As all the department have their own set of policies and procedures, but to achieve the organisation goals the activities of various departments. have to be coordinated.
- **Growing specialization** - Modern business has become increasingly complex as various functions are to be performed by specialists. Specialisation, brings about need for more coordination because of diversity of tasks to be performed.

Value of human relations in management:

In any organisation, relationships between employees and management are extremely important. The process of teaching employees, addressing their needs, developing a working culture, and resolving disagreements between co-workers or between co-workers and management is known as human relations. Understanding some of the ways that human connections can affect a company's costs, competitiveness, and long-term economic viability helps to emphasise their significance.

Establishing and maintaining fruitful business partnerships necessitates the development of excellent human relation abilities. Managerial attention and good communication usually lead to higher levels of productivity and job satisfaction. Working in groups and teams is achievable with good human relations abilities. One of the advantages of a company climate that encourages open and honest communication is the increased opportunity for understanding among different groups. Establishing a respectful approach toward employees as human beings may result in better working conditions and increased loyalty to the organisation.

Bottom line: **Communication, conflict resolution, multitasking, negotiation and organization** are all vital to human relations. Leaders who develop these skills are on their way to successfully implementing human relations management practices.

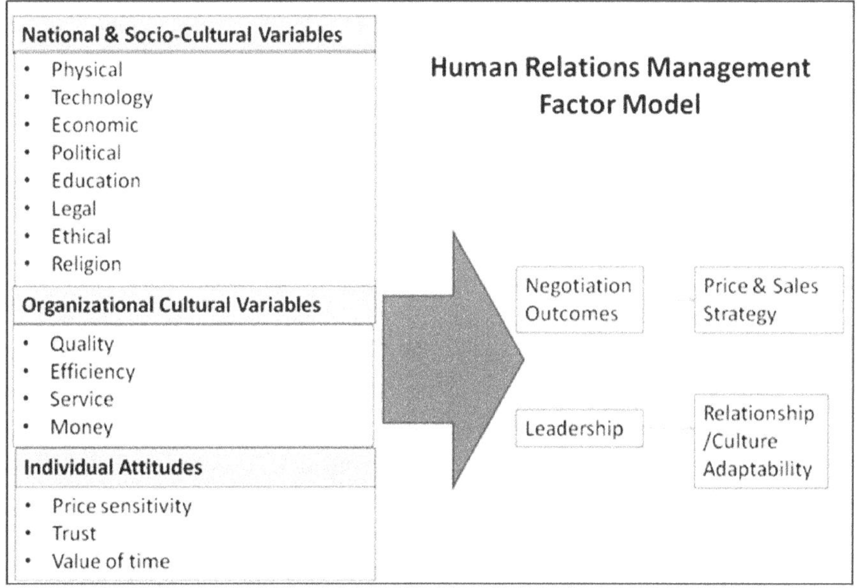

Source – Management study

Relationships between employees and management are of substantial value in any workplace. Human relations is the process of training employees, addressing their needs, fostering a workplace culture and resolving conflicts between different employees or between employees and management. Understanding some of the the ways that human relations can impact the costs, competitiveness and long-term economic sustainability of a business helps to underscore their importance.

Human relations abilities

By creating key human relations abilities, administrators and representatives both can fabricate and keep up with more grounded connections inside a labor force and keep a positive workplace. Here are the most basic human relations abilities:

- **Correspondence:**

Correspondence is fundamental in any workplace. By having the option to discuss successfully with representatives, you can guarantee that workers feel esteemed and spurred in the work they're doing. By passing messages on to other people and tuning in fully intent on understanding, supervisors can sustain sensations of trust.

- Pioneers ought to adjust the language to the circumstance.
- **Sympathy**

Sympathy is another significant human relations ability that permits you to show certified interest in grasping the sentiments or difficulties that others are encountering. Sympathy permits you to take a gander at a circumstance according to their viewpoint and assist them with feeling they can trust you. By taking a gander at a circumstance according to their perspective, you can show them sympathy and all the more effectively find answers for issues they might be having, if proper. This can reinforce the relationship you have with them.

- **Compromise**

Struggle can happen in the working environment when you have an enormous number of colleagues with various character types, objectives and perspectives. Administrators, then, should have advanced compromise abilities. Whenever struggle emerges, you should have the option to pay attention to the singular points of view so every individual included feels that they are being heard and perceived. When the realities are introduced, you then work with the gatherings to think of an answer that everybody is alright with. By creating solid compromise abilities, you can really assist with fortifying the connections of representatives in your group and keep up with or reestablish concordance in the work environment.

- **Performing various tasks**

Pioneers should have the option to deal with different, now and again contending, needs while remaining on-cutoff time. They additionally are frequently hindered with questions and face various startling errands consistently. They are liable for ensuring that their own work is finished and furthermore for guaranteeing crafted by their time is being finished as quickly as possibly.

- **Association**

Pioneers should have the option to deal with their time really and work effectively, particularly while they're chipping away at numerous needs that are time-delicate. Association influences all region of a workplace. It incorporates a chief's capacity to keep their actual work area coordinated as well as sort out their cycles so they are productive and come by the ideal outcomes. Administrators are ordinarily liable for keeping up with worker records and finishing up administrative work. Association abilities are basic to have the option to deal with these obligations.

- **Exchange**

Exchange abilities are significant for assisting different gatherings with arriving at pleasant terms. Chiefs are many times liable for aiding agree among sellers and their organization, arranging work offers or even overseeing contradicting perspectives. The reflecting methodology portrayed above can assist directors with being more viable arbitrators.

- **Stress the executives**

Since pioneers are liable for dealing with the assumptions for partners, dealing with a group of individuals and focusing on their own work to accomplish organization targets, they are occasionally confronted with distressing circumstances. Therefore, supervisors should be furnished with compelling pressure the board abilities and have the option to resist the urge to panic under tension. By effectively involving pressure the executives strategies and demonstrating them for their group, they can assist with keeping a quiet workplace, in any event, when a group is under elevated degrees of tension.

Benefits of Human relations
The various benefits are depicted beneath

- The human relations approach is thought of as worthwhile for an association as it lifts work environment as well as worker confidence level
- The program increments representative support in the dynamic interaction
- A fundamental benefit of the program is to further develop correspondence in the work environment
- The upside of this program in the association is to make less generic working circumstances
- The program is viewed as beneficial for an association as it assists with supporting position fulfillment
- It helps with further developing consumer loyalty on the grounds that the connection between the representatives and clients will in general be sound and impending
- The program supports worker strengthening, and for this reason it demonstrates helpful for an association
- The goal of the program is to kill representative disappointment and non-attendance in the work environment. It is thought of as beneficial as it brings about a lower pace of representative turnover and a higher pace of worker maintenance
- The program makes progress toward giving preparation and improving valuable open doors

CONCLUSION

Creating relationship abilities in people is a need in these advanced times for a useful business relationship. It prompts genuine correspondence, better comprehension, and a positive working condition.

It is an essential interaction whose object is to fulfil individual necessities and hierarchical objectives.

CHAPTER IV

PROJECT MANAGEMENT: TIME OF PROGRESS CHART, BAR CHART, GANTT CHART, CPM & PERT, ALLOCATION OF TIME TO VARIOUS ACTIVITIES

Introduction:

A project is a set of agreed-upon actions with a distinct beginning, middle, and end point. These operations work together to create commercial products or services in accordance with a business case approved by senior management.

Project management organises and controls the project environment so that the agreed-upon activities produce the appropriate products or services that meet the customer's expectations.

Projects are temporary structures that must be appropriately managed and regulated in order to achieve their stated goals. They are typically administered in environments where funding and resources are both limited and competitive.

Project management is a necessary skill for various occupations and situations in our lives. If you need to handle projects at work or at home but aren't a properly trained project manager, Introduction to Project Management is a great place to start. It's also appropriate if you're planning a project in the near future and want to learn and apply important project management information and abilities.

To successfully complete a project, it's critical to first define what the project is and what the expected outcomes are. We will show you how to use the course to examine and comprehend your goals from the start of your project, as well as to consider all of the variables that may affect its implementation. From start to finish, you'll learn how to plan, scope, schedule, cost, and manage your project step by step. Because the success of any project is dependent on the people who deliver it, the course also allows you to learn how to effectively communicate, manage people, and use leadership abilities to complete your own project.

Whether your project is huge or little, you will learn practical ways to employ project management abilities in Introduction to Project Management. Join us to learn how project management approaches can help you with your own initiatives.

Source: Project Smart

Time of progress chart, bar chart, Gantt chart, CPM & PERT:

You must be smart, sincere, hardworking, and multi-skilled to succeed in project management. However, there is one more trait that you must possess in order to be a good project manager: the ability to employ the appropriate project management tools and methodologies.

Data visualisation tools are one of the many tools you may utilise to properly manage your tasks. These tools use charts to present you with useful information about your projects, allowing you to steer projects in the proper direction while assuring higher-quality deliveries.

What is the definition of a project management chart?

A project management chart is a graphical representation of project information. You can use many sorts of project management charts to minimise bottlenecks and make better judgments while working on projects. These diagrams can also be used to streamline project processes, efficiently manage resources, and improve time management. The most prominent feature of project management charts is that they make complex project data easy to comprehend.

Project managers use many sorts of charts to examine and monitor various aspects of their projects. While some project management charts, such as Gantt charts, are widely used, others, such as Pareto charts and control charts, are rarely employed.

Why Do You Need Project Management Charts?

There is a restricted set of data that you must observe during the life cycle of simple and small scale enterprises. However, as the projects become more sophisticated, you will need to keep track of an increasing amount of data. Project management charts can be extremely useful in this situation.

The most significant benefit of using project management charts is that they allow you to quickly examine and extract relevant project information. These graphs organise data in a logical manner, making it easier to examine project data.

You might be interested in the following important advantages of project management charts:

- Eliminates the need to travel back and forth to collect project data, saving a significant amount of time.
- Assist you in staying informed about the project's progress.
- Encourage team members to work together.
- Allow you to have better knowledge and clarity of the project.
- Project management becomes straightforward and efficient.
- Assist in improving the project strategy and dealing with unexpected challenges.

Before we go any further, it's important to note that the aforementioned advantages are found in most project management charts. However, you should be aware that each project management chart has its own set of advantages that make it appropriate for usage in a specific context or project.

Now, it's time to get familiar with the project management charts that are highly popular:

1. **Gantt Chart –**

    Gantt charts are the most common project management charts used by modern firms and managers to keep track of their projects. The temporal view of your projects is provided through a Gantt chart. It allows you to see how different project tasks/activities are connected to one another and how they fit into the overall project timeline.

Gantt Chart

Task Name	Q1 2019			Q2 2019		Q3 2019
	Jan 19	Feb 19	Mar 19	Apr 19	Jun 19	Jul 19
Planning						
Research						
Design						
Implementation						
Follow up						

Source: ProofHub

A Gantt chart is a simplified version of a bar chart that is simple to understand. The project's duties are represented on the vertical axis, while the time length is represented on the horizontal axis.

Many popular online project management tools, such as ProofHub, now include interactive Gantt charts to help you keep track of all your tasks.

The nicest part of using an online Gantt chart tool is that it is simple to use and allows for team participation. You may organise projects, schedule and assign tasks, define task dependencies, correlate project milestones with tasks, and track progress using online Gantt charts. You can also determine a project's critical route, which allows you to estimate the project's duration.

Gantt charts are a subtle approach to organise all of the important project data in one place and boost your team's efficiency. Furthermore, these charts can be used to manage your projects utilising the critical path method (CPM).

1. **PERT Chart –**

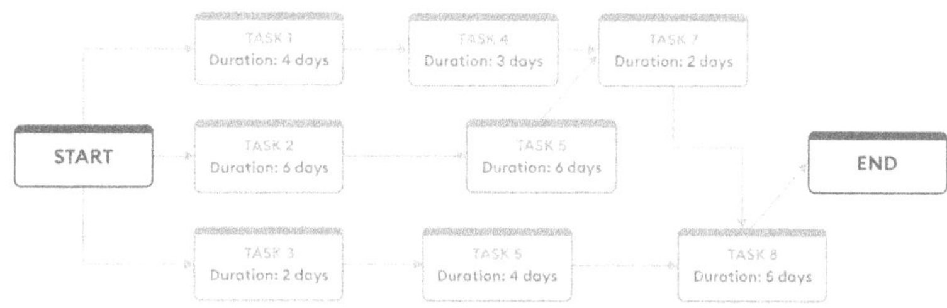

Source: ProofHub

Another prominent project management chart is the PERT chart, which is used to schedule, control, and monitor project work. The abbreviation PERT stands for Program Evaluation and Review Technique, and it is one of the most widely utilised project management approaches across a number of industries.

A PERT chart is a network diagram that depicts the activities and milestones of a project. Interestingly, the PERT and CPM approaches have many similarities, and both are commonly used to manage projects simultaneously.

The most important distinction between the two methodologies is that CPM is effective for managing project activities with fixed durations, whereas PERT is best for managing activities with variable durations.

A PERT chart has circles and arrows on it. The circles represent project activities, and the arrows show how the activities progress. A PERT chart can be used to identify both critical and non-critical project activities. The chart also includes information about parallel tasks that you can do at the same time to accelerate project development without placing too much strain on resources.

When utilising PERT charts for the first time, you might find them a little confusing. However, understanding them and utilising their potential to productively arrange initiatives will not take long.

Advantages

• This technique helps the management to plan the best possible use resouces to a given goal within the time and cost limitations.

• It helps management to handle the uncertainties involved in the program.

• It process for the right action point and at right time in the organization.

• It provides information on existence of slack period between activies and what avtivities are crucial in terms of time to complete project.

• It gives a basis of obtaining the necessary facts for decision-making.

• PERT allows a large amount of data to be presented in a well-organized diagram known as network from which both the executor and customer can make joint decisions.

Limitations

• The basic difficulty comes in the way of time estimate for the completion of activities because activites are non-repetitive type.

• The technique does not consider resources required at various stages of the project.

• Use of this technique for active control of a project requires frequent updating a revising the PERT calculations and this provesquite a costly affair. When PERT applied properly it helps to do the following jobs effectively.

• Cut project cost and reduce time.

• Coordinate and expedite planning. • Eliminate slack(idle) time.

• Cut time required for routine decisions,but allow more time for critical decision-makings

2. Critical path method: - CPM is a technique which is used for the projects where the time needed for completion of project is already known. It is majorly used for determining the approximate time within which a project can be completed. The critical path is the largest path in project management which always provide minimum time taken for completion of project.

Critical path method is one of the frequently used techniques in project planning. A typical project has many tasks involving lots of different people so project managers have a hard time keeping track of things. It is far too easy for certain activities to fall behind and get lost in the sea of endless jobs. These forgotten tasks and errors in planning can severely affect the timescale of the whole project.

A late project will cost money and lead to unhappy customers and bosses. Critical path method in project management helps managers figure out two very important things. How long it will take to complete the project and what are the critical tasks that must be completed before starting other dependent tasks. The best way for project managers to avoid poor planning is to incorporate the critical path method in their diagrams. Having this as a diagram makes it easy to visualize the important tasks of a project. This is really helpful for managers and makes it easier for the project team to visualize and plan their work accordingly. The main aim is to produce a visual of the entire project broken down into smaller activities which are vital to the completion of the entire project.

All of the activities which are added to the network diagram are the ones which have to be completed on time. By adding them on to a diagram it is possible to see how long each section will take. This is essential when it comes to predicting the timescale of the project. The benefits of applying each of the set time critical and essential activities to a diagram include:

- Predicting the time each activity will take and offering a timescale to the client
- Seeing how each section is important to the progress of the rest of the plan
- Assigning the right team and department to their corresponding tasks

S. no.	PERT	CPM
1.	PERT is that technique of project management which is used to manage uncertain (i.e., time is not known) activities of any project.	CPM is that technique of project manager which is used to manage only certain (i.e., time is known) activities of any project.
2.	It is event-oriented technique which means that network is constructed on the basis of event.	It is activity-oriented technique which means that network is constructed on the basis of activities.
3.	It is a probability model.	It is a deterministic model.
4.	It majorly focuses on time as meeting time target or estimation of percent completion is more important.	It majorly focuses on time-cost trade off as minimizing cost is more important.
5.	It is appropriate for high precision time estimation.	It is appropriate for reasonable time estimation.
6.	It has non- repetitive nature of job.	It has repetitive nature of job.
7.	There is no chance of crashing as there is no certainty of time.	There may be crashing because of certain time boundation.

3. Flow Chart –

It's challenging to manage projects with several processes and a complicated flow of operations. When dealing with intricate projects, a flowchart is the greatest answer for simplifying them and making your life easier.

A flowchart is a graphical representation of the project workflow for those who are unfamiliar. It encompasses all actions and procedures that occur between the project's initiation and completion. The sequence of events and their connections are depicted using boxes and figures of various shapes, as well as arrows.

It's challenging to manage projects with several processes and a complicated flow of operations. When dealing with intricate projects, a flowchart is the greatest answer for simplifying them and making your life easier.

A flowchart is a graphical representation of the project workflow for those who are unfamiliar. It encompasses all actions and procedures that occur between the project's initiation and completion. The sequence of events and their connections are depicted using boxes and figures of various shapes, as well as arrows.

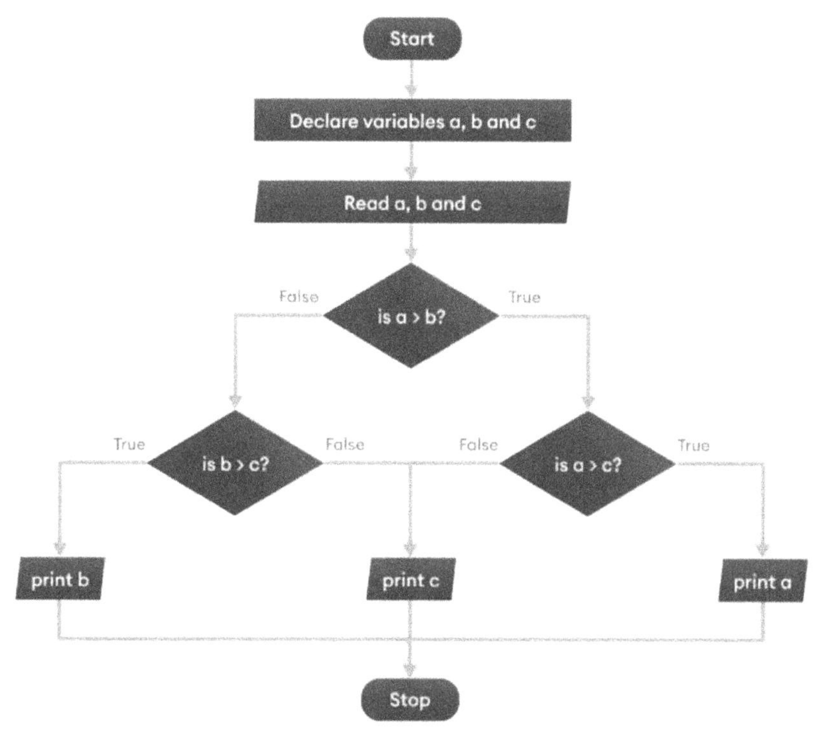

Source: ProofHub

Flowcharts are an excellent way to outline the logic that will be used in your projects and share it with others, such as team members, clients, stakeholders, and so on. A flowchart presents a clear picture of the project's goals as well as an overview of what will happen during the various project events and phases.

Flowcharts are particularly successful when utilised for small projects, as a manager should be aware. Creating flowcharts for huge projects with a lot of processes and sequences, on the other hand, is impossible. Flowcharts are used in conjunction with Gantt charts for large-scale projects to improve project management.

4. Bar Chart –

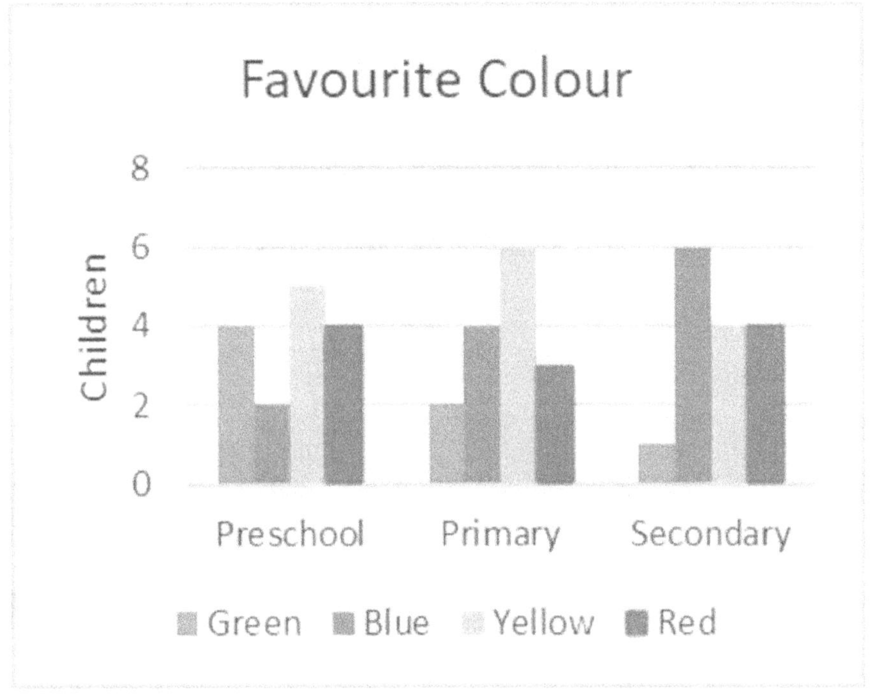

Source: ProofHub

Bar charts are widely used in project management because they are simple, adaptable, and easy to understand. These charts are used in project management to visualise a wide range of project data, from billable and non-billable work hours to the number of completed and pending tasks.

A conventional bar chart includes two axes, one indicating the different categories to compare and the other showing the comparison parameter. Although bars can be plotted horizontally or vertically, horizontal bar charts are more common.

You may need to visualise some data while managing a project, such as how your staff distributes their work hours across multiple projects. You can rapidly obtain key project information using bar charts.

Bar charts are used in almost all prominent project management software to illustrate some aspect of the project data. As the project continues and new project activities occur, the software automatically creates and modifies bar charts.

Planning of activities:

Effective project time management requires project planning and scheduling activities.

It is the initial phase in every project's planning stage, and the procedures should be followed as a form of pre-project planning art. The second step of project time management is project activity planning, and the third step is generating project implementation schedules.

The following four steps should be considered and can be conducted efficiently with project management software such as Sinnaps in order to carry out effective project planning activities:

- Define the project's many activities.
- Define the interdependencies and linkages between activities.
- Estimate the resources needed.
- Calculate the length of each activity.

Project Planning List:

For each type of project, the activity planning stage is critical. Take a look at the following list of project planning tasks for activity planning and sequencing:

- Determine the project's specifications.
- Find every database.
- Calculate cost estimates
- Examine the risk assessment again.
- Define and recognise key success factors.
- Create a project charter.

- Make a thorough project plan.
- Start the project.

Project Planning Activities:

Process planning is organising functions and operations in order to provide a detailed plan and/or instructions for fabricating a part or completing a project. The planning process begins with engineering drawings, material lists, and specifications. These define the operation sequences, work centres, tools, and standards that must be satisfied as part of software engineering project planning operations. This becomes a critical input into a product's manufacturing process, outlining operations for any production activity control measures as well as determining the required resources for capacity planning.

Project teams will benefit immensely from activity planning in project management, as well as process plans that provide specific outlines of task instructions. Process activity planning provides vital step-by-step instructions that team members must comprehend in order to do activities correctly and to a higher standard.

Allocation of time to various activities:

The act of devoting different hours of one's day, week, or year to different activities, particularly those that fall under the categories of labour and leisure.

We've all had problems with time management at work. You wake up full of hope and optimism, knowing that not only will you fulfil all of your deadlines, but you'll also go to the gym and prepare a nutritious home-cooked supper.

After that, life happens. You leave late, get stuck in traffic, and arrive at your desk already frustrated. When you sit down to finish that job you've been putting off for weeks, you realise you have back-to-back meetings till noon—and you're already late for the first one. You finally leave the last meeting and begin reading emails when you are called into a meeting with the vice president. You've been asked to fulfil a last-minute request by him. He estimates that it will only take an hour. Make it three.

The good news is that those seemingly illusive lost hours of the day can be reclaimed. It's all about personal time management—controlling your time rather than allowing it to control you. To get you started, here are some work time management strategies.

1. Figure out how you're currently spending your time.
2. Create a daily schedule—and stick with it.
3. Prioritize wisely.
4. Group similar tasks together.
5. Avoid the urge to multitask.
6. Assign time limits to tasks.
7. Build in buffers.
8. Learn to say no.
9. Get organized.
10. Eliminate distractions.

When you manage your time well, you not only get more done, but you also have more time to do things you enjoy. Working on a task with no predetermined time frame will have a better effect than working on a task with a particular time slot, like 1 hour.

- **Allocation of time to various activities**

1. The Pomodoro Technique
Toggle says that this technique can be a solution to your worries if you have noticed that your co-workers or employees get easily distracted.

All you have to do is to persuade them to set the timer.

The technique distributes your workload more evenly throughout the day and helps you keep your focus on the task.

- Take your to-do list.
- Choose the task you want to complete.
- Set your timer for a 25-minute block (aka one Pomodoro).
- Don't multitask, don't interrupt your working process with small distractions. Work solely on the task of your choice.
- When the time is up, you have earned yourself a 5-minute break.
- After 4 cycles of Pomodoro's, take a longer break – 20-ish minutes.

2. Task Batching
If you are constantly multitasking but realize that at the end of the day you haven't fully completed not even one of your to-dos, the task batching

technique can be the right one for you. Grab your to-do list and a bunch of highlighters and get to work.

The goal is to find a few tasks in your list that are similar and could be done at once. With the help of different highlighters, you will be able to group activities into categories based on their similarities. You might be used to tackling urgent matters first and this could change the order a bit, but it will actually make you more productive than before if you tend to get off track easily.

3. Golden hours

It is impossible to stay motivated at all times. A person is constantly influenced by other circumstances, moods, feelings, and thoughts. Therefore, you shouldn't judge yourself harshly if you are lacking focus or motivation. This time management activity is quite similar to the Circadian Rhythm with the sole difference that you can do it for personal purposes, instead of for trying to build the perfect team. Start a journal where you document your workdays. Try to keep it for a week or so.

4. 80/20 rule

The 80/20 rule, also known as the Pareto Principle, is a time allocation technique that suggests that our daily tasks are divided into 2 sections – vital and trivial. The vital tasks take up 20% of our to-do list, while the trivial, simpler, tasks are 80%. It is important to understand this rule since it can be applied to everything in our life. Including handling our businesses.

5. Automate your tasks

I bet you're fed up with dealing with repetitive manual tasks that a machine could easily do for you. All you need is the right software or a set of tools. The process of automation could reduce operational costs, increase reliability, and give you more time which you can spend on something of greater importance.

6. Prioritize tasks

I already mentioned the 80/20 rule. It is an illustration of the ratio of unimportant to important activities.

In order to be efficient, you should prioritize and complete important tasks first.

They might take more time; they might be more difficult to tackle. However, at the end of the day, they will be way more beneficial in comparison to the rest.

Personal management and industrial relations- recruitments, selection, training, wage and salary administration related to small

industries:

Personnel management is the administrative function of estimating and classifying human resource requirements in order to achieve organisational goals through people at work and their interpersonal interactions.

Personnel management entails techniques for ensuring the correct amount of employees, the right mix of talent, training, and job performance.

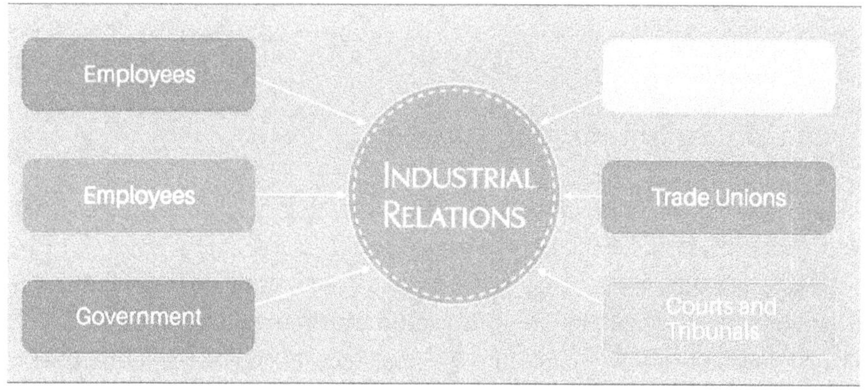

Source: Danshaw Consulting

"Employees Management is the planning, organising, directing, and managing of the procurement, development, compensation, integration, and maintenance, and separation of personnel to the end that individual, organisational, and societal objectives are achieved," according to Edwin B. Flippo.

Personnel management and industrial relations are two related topics that deal with many aspects of the relationship between an organization's management and its employees, as well as the relationship between vested parties such as labour unions. Personnel management differs from industrial relations in that the former is more concerned with recruiting, training, and effective employee relations, whilst the latter is more concerned with trade unions and other forms of organised labour in connection to employment concerns. In this view, the relationship between personnel management and labour relations can be described as a common concern for the well-being of employees and other forms of labour.

CHAPTER V

WAGE AND SALARY ADMINISTRATION, RECRUITING, SELECTION, AND TRAINING, METHODS AND TECHNIQUES OF MINIMIZING COST

Wage and salary administration

Wage and salary administration refers to the process of determining wage and salary levels and structures in organisational contexts.

Wage and salary: - A salary is the regular payment made by an employer to an employee for employment. It can be expressed monthly or annually, but it is most commonly paid monthly, particularly to white collar workers, managers, directors, and professionals.

Wages are hourly payments for labour services performed on a regular basis, whereas salaries are weekly, monthly, or annual payments for the same services rendered on a weekly, monthly, or annual basis, expressed in weekly, monthly, or annual rates.

As a result, the term "wage" typically refers to payments based on the number of hours worked, and it can vary depending on the number of hours actually worked.

Compensation administration includes determining wage rates, administering wage regulations, and ensuring that employees are satisfied with their earnings and wage rates.

In reality, one of the key duties of modern labour management is pay and salary administration.

Significance of wage & salary administration:

Wage & salaries have two different purposes from point of employers & employees.

(i) Employers perceive as a cost of business effort and attempt to reduce it. But they also realise that it is not possible because of these reasons:

(a) Wage & salary are essential to attract and retain an effective work force.

(b) Wage and salary are required to motivate, employees for positive attitudes and better performance.

(c) Employees have to be provided compensation for service rendered by them to the organisation.

(ii) Employees consider wage as a means for satisfying their need to maintain their standard. They also want it equitable with similar skills for doing similar work.

Principles of Wage & Salary administration:

1. Wage & salary plans and policies should be sufficiently flexible.

2. Job evaluation must be done scientifically.

3. Wage & salary administration plans. Must always be consistent with overall organisation plans & programmes.

4. Wage & salary administration plans and programmes should be in conformity with the social & economic objectives of the country like attainment of equality of income distribution and controlling inflationary trends. Wages & salary administration plans and programmes should be responsive to the changing local and national conditions. The plans should simply & expedite other administration processes

What is the difference between recruiting, selection, and training?

Recruitment refers to the process of determining whether or not an organisation needs to hire someone up until the application forms for the position arrive at the organisation. The processes involved in selecting a qualified candidate from a pool of candidates to fill a position are referred to as selection.

What role do personnel selection and training have in a company's success?

An effective recruitment and selection policy not only meets the job needs, but also guarantees that an organization's commitment to equal opportunity for all employees is upheld. Following such a policy will allow you to hire the top applicants for your company.

What's the difference between selection and recruitment?

Recruitment is the process of actively seeking and hiring candidates for a job position. Selection is the process of selecting appropriate applications from a list of candidates that have been shortlisted. It's a campaign to increase the number of candidates in the pool. It's a process of whittling down the applicant pool until we find the perfect match.

Difference between recruitment and selection

Basis	Recruitment	Selection
Meaning	It is the process of stimulating people to apply for a vacant job position in the organisation.	It is the process of selecting the best candidate from those who have applied for the job.
Objective	The objective of recruitment is create a pool of eligible candidates for the purpose of selection.	The objective of selection is to get the best candidate selected for the job.
Nature	It is a positive process as it attracts people towards the organisation.	It is a negative process as it involves rejection of candidates at every stage of it.
Sequence	It takes place before selection.	It takes place after recruitment.

quora.com

Recruitment: - Recruitment is the process of examining a vacant position in the organisation and attracting potential candidates to apply for the same, within an appropriate time and at a desirable cost. It is the introductory stage where a job applicant gets to know about the vacancy, and the organisation identifies the candidate's profile.

Selection: - **Project Selection** is a process to assess each **project** idea and select the **project** with the highest priority. **Selection** of **projects** is based on: Benefits: A measure of the positive outcomes of the **project**. These are often described as "the reasons why you are undertaking the **project**".

Training: - Training aimed at developing entrepreneurial competence in potential individuals is called entrepreneurial training. Motivating probable entrepreneurs, assisting. these individuals in endeavour to do the appropriate activities and enterprises, improving their enterprise development skills, and facilitating them to make economically and technically feasible project reports are the main activities of entrepreneurial training programmes.

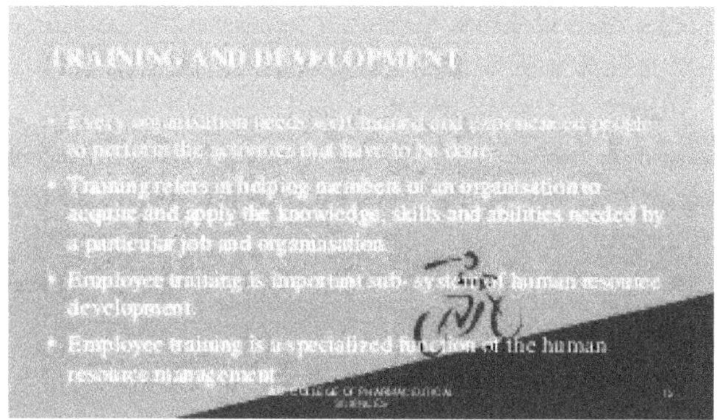

slideshare.net

Costing

Methods and Techniques of Minimizing Cost:

You'll learn everything you need to know about costing strategies and approaches. The strategies and processes used in cost estimation are referred to as costing methods or kinds.

For different industries, there are different costing methodologies. The costing method to be employed in a specific business is determined by the type of production and industry.

In addition to the costing methods, there are several costing approaches that can be used in conjunction with any of the methods. These strategies are used for managerial control and policy purposes.

Some of the methods of costing are: 1. Job Costing 2. Contract Costing 3. Cost Plus Costing 4. Batch Costing 5. Process Costing 6. Operation Costing 7. Unit Costing 8. Operating Costing 9. Departmental Costing 10. Multiple Costing.

Some of the techniques of costing are: 1. Budgetary Control 2. Standard Costing 3. Marginal Costing 4. Life Style Costing 5. Target Costing 6. Activity-Based Costing.

Methods of Costing:

The various methods of costing are as follows:

Job Costing –

This is a strategy in which costs are independently collected and aggregated for each job. This is done because each project requires a unique mark and has its own identity, making it necessary to examine and divide expenditures for each job independently.

Batch Costing –

In this strategy, manufacturers that must generate a large number of parts in order to manufacture a product produce each part in batches. Products are organised in convenient batches, and each batch is handled as a single project with its own cost. A bicycle factory, for example, may build 10,000 handles at a time before moving on to other parts in separate batches. Batch costing is the method of determining the cost of each batch independently.

Process Costing –

It is a system in which costs are gathered and aggregated by department or process, and then the cost of each department or process is divided by the quantity of production to arrive at the cost per unit. Paper, soap, textiles, chemicals, sugar, and food processing products all benefit from this technology.

Operation Costing –

Process costing has been refined and applied in a more thorough manner. Instead of pricing by process, this method involves costing by operation. To create an article, many operations are required. This procedure is more precise and controlled.

Single (Unit or Output) Costing –

When production is uniform and consists of only one product or two or three types of similar products with only minor differences in size, shape, or quality, this method is used. The data is given in the form of a cost sheet, which is a statement.

Operating Costing –

Operating costing is a costing system used when a company does not create tangible commodities but instead provides a service. This is used to calculate the expenses of services provided by airlines, railways, highways, hospitals, power plants, and other entities. For example, a transportation company wants to know how much it costs to move one tonne of products per kilometre.

Multiple Costing –

When the finished product comprises of a number of independent elements, such as a radio set, a car, or a bicycle, this method is used. The cost of each part must be determined, and then the cost of putting the pieces together must be calculated. The total cost of the final product will include the cost of all parts as well as the cost of assembly.

Uniform costing –

Uniform costing occurs when a group of companies in the same industry agree to adopt the same costing techniques. This strategy tries to provide a uniform costing mechanism so that performance in multiple undertakings may be compared to the benefit of all participating units.

Techniques of Costing:

Following are the main techniques of costing:

Marginal Costing –

It is the determination of marginal cost, which distinguishes between fixed and variable costs. The determination of marginal costs and the effect of changes in volume or type of output on profit by distinguishing between fixed and variable costs.

Standard Costing –

The creation and application of standard costs, as well as their comparison to real costs and study of variance to determine their causes and points of incidence. This allows management to look into the causes of the discrepancies and take the required corrective action.

Direct Costing –

It is the practise of charging all direct costs into variable and fixed costs related to operations, processes, or goods, and then writing off all other costs against profits as they emerge.

Absorption Costing –

Full costing is another term for absorption costing. It's a costing method in which all manufacturing costs (both fixed and variable) are accounted for as cost of production and utilised to calculate the cost of items manufactured and inventories. Fixed manufacturing expenses are included in the actual production costs.

Uniform Costing –

It refers to the use of the same costing ideas and methods across all business units for cost comparison and control. "The application of the same costing concepts and perhaps techniques by many ventures," according to CIMA. This allows you to compare one business's performance to another's and benefit from whoever has more expertise and performs better.

Budgetary Control –

A budget is used to keep track of and coordinate the operations of a company. A budget is a numerical or financial statement made for a specific time period. Budgetary control is the application of a comprehensive budgeting system to assist management in planning, coordinating, and regulating operations. One of the most significant control mechanisms is budgetary control.

CHAPTER VI

MARKETING- CONCEPT AND FUNCTIONS, MARKETING MIX, PRODUCT PLANNING, SALESMANSHIP AND ITS PRINCIPLES,SOURCES OF FINANCE

Marketing- concept and functions, marketing mix, product planning, salesmanship and its principles:

Marketing Concept, is a business philosophy that opposes the three business orientations listed above. In the 1950s, the core beliefs of the movement became clear. It asserts that the key to attaining the firm's organisational goals (selling company goals) is for the company to be more effective than competitors at generating, delivering, and communicating customer value to its chosen target consumers. Target market, customer needs, integrated marketing, and profitability are the four pillars of the marketing concept.

The Marketing Concept is fascinated with the idea of meeting a customer's demands through the use of a product as a solution to a customer's problem (needs).

The Marketing Concept is a key shift in today's corporate culture that lays the groundwork for achieving competitive advantage.

The 6 Essential Marketing Concepts

1. **Production Concept**
2. **Product Concept**
3. **Selling Concept**
4. **Marketing Concept**
5. **Societal Marketing Concept**
6. **Holistic Marketing Concept**

Source: TeamWorkZ

Marketing Management Philosophies or 5 Marketing Concepts are:

1. Production Concept,
2. Product Concept,
3. Selling Concept,
4. Marketing Concept,
5. Societal Marketing Concept.

Production Concept -

"Consumers will prefer things that are available and highly affordable," says the production philosophy. This is one of the most ancient marketing management orientations for sellers.

Companies that follow this approach face the risk of narrowing their emphasis too much on their operations and losing sight of the real goal.

The production concept can frequently lead to marketing myopia. Management is focused on increasing the efficiency of production and distribution. The production notion is still a valuable philosophy in some contexts.

If a company decides to operate under this philosophy, it will aim to reduce manufacturing costs by making the process more efficient. Furthermore, in order for its items to be popular with consumers, it will aim to expand its distribution as much as possible.

If two scenarios exist, this production concept is judged to be appropriate.

- One, when a product's demand surpasses its supply. This is evident in markets with a high price sensitivity and a tight budget. In such circumstances, consumers will be more concerned with possessing the goods than with its quality or features. As a result, producers will be motivated to increase their outputs.
- Two, if the manufacturing expenses are prohibitively high, people will be hesitant to purchase the goods. The corporation concentrates all of its efforts here on increasing manufacturing volume and developing technology in order to reduce expenses.

Reduced production costs aid in the firm's reduction, which in turn aids in the expansion of the market. As a result, a corporation can attempt to establish a dominant position in the market in which it operates.

This notion is widely used in service organisations such as hospitals. The application of this principle in service firms such as hospitals has also been questioned, as it may lead to a decline in service quality.

Example of a Production Concept:
You see, the market is swamped with low-cost Chinese products on Amazon and in retail stores. Everything from China's low-cost plastic product is currently in your shopping cart.

Vivo, a Chinese smartphone manufacturer, is the best example of the production concept. Their phones can be found in practically every Asian country. You can walk into any Vivo store in Asia and walk away with the newest and most advanced smartphone.

Product Concept –
Consumers will prefer products with the highest quality, performance, and unique features, according to the product concept. Here. Continuous product enhancements are the emphasis of marketing tactics.

Product quality and improvement are critical components of marketing strategy, and in some cases, they are the only component. Marketing myopia could result from focusing solely on the company's products.

More and more industries adopted mass production techniques during the first three decades of the twentieth century. By the early 1930s, the supply of produced products had outstripped demand.

Manufacturers were confronted with surplus capacity and fierce rivalry for customers. They began to realise that buyers prefer well-made items and are prepared to pay more for product extras, and the product concept began to take shape in many manufacturers' minds.

Consumers will prefer products that are superior in quality, performance, innovative features, designs, and so on, according to the product concept.

This marketing strategy was supposed to be straightforward: whomever delivered a standard product at the lowest price would win. A company that follows this ideology strives to improve its products' quality, performance, and any other observable aspect.

Followers of the product concept philosophy are always improving their products.

Consumers prefer well-made products that are superior to competing products in the above-mentioned qualities, according to proponents of this philosophy.

Many product-oriented businesses design their goods with little or no input from their target markets.

They believe that their engineers or designers understand product design or enhancement factors better than their customers.

They also do not compare their products to those of competitors in order to make improvements. They became enamoured with "love affair" and acted unrealistically like people do when in love with someone of the other sex.

"How can the public know what kind of car they want unless they see what is available?" a GM executive once stated.

Engineers design and develop the product first, then production produces it, finance prices it, and marketing and sales attempt to sell it.

Many marketers still believe this premise, and it has such sway over some that they have forgotten that the market is shifting in a different direction. This concept has very little room for marketing.

The product is the major focus here. As a result, it's clear that in the product concept, management fails to recognise what business it's in, resulting in marketing myopia – or a lack of understanding of marketing's role.

Example of a Product Concept:

Assume a corporation produces the highest-quality floppy disc. But what if a consumer requires a floppy disc?

She or he will require a means of storing the information. A USB flash drive, SD memory cards, portable hard discs, and other similar devices can be used to accomplish this. Instead of focusing on making the finest floppy disc, the corporation should focus on addressing the data storage demands of its customers.

When it comes to high-quality items, Apple is at the top of the list. Their products are so superb that they establish industry norms and trends.

Logitech produces high-quality computer accessories like keyboards, mice, and webcams. Although these high-quality products are more expensive, consumers continue to buy them, and they receive essentially free advertising from independent reviewers.

Selling Concept –

The selling idea holds the thought "purchasers won't buy enough of the company's items except if it embraces a huge scope selling and advancement exertion."

Here the administration centres around making deals exchanges as opposed to on building long haul, productive client connections.

All in all, the point is to sell what the organization makes as opposed to making what the market needs. Such a forceful selling program conveys extremely high dangers.

In selling idea, the advertiser accepts that clients will be persuaded to purchasing the item will like it; in the event that they could do without it, they will perhaps fail to remember their mistake and get it once more at a later time. This is typically an extremely poor and expensive supposition.

Ordinarily the selling idea is polished with unsought merchandise. Unsought products are that purchasers don't typically consider purchasing, like protection or blood gifts.

These businesses should be great at finding possibilities and selling them on an item's advantages.

The selling idea likewise created simultaneously, and the item idea created nevertheless prevalent in numerous businesses.

The economic crisis of the early 20s in America demonstrated that delivering an adequate number of merchandise or quality products is not any more an issue. The issue is to sell those items.

Creating quality items doesn't be guaranteed to ensure its deal. During this period, the essential job of selling, promoting, and other showcasing capacities was coordinated really, and the selling idea appeared.

As characterized by Philip Kotler, it holds that purchasers, whenever left alone, will customarily not buy enough of the association's items. Forceful selling and advancement exercises can ensure deals.

As indicated by him, purchasers regularly show purchasing dormancy and in some cases impervious to purchasing and must be affected by various means so they are consented to purchase. The organization's capacity is to impact customers by utilizing all potential deals strategies so they are urged to purchase more.

As Kotler says, the selling idea is polished most forcefully with unsought products, those merchandise that purchasers ordinarily don't consider purchasing, like protection, reference books, and burial service plots.

This idea is for the most part utilized on account of overcapacity, where a firm needs to sell what it makes. It begins with the mark of creation, which centres around items, and its point is to procure benefit through expanded deals volume, and the means utilized are selling and advancing.

Showcasing, in its actual sense, actually doesn't get an essential situation in this idea. Advertising, here, for sure in light of hard selling. In moving merchandise from makers to buyers, the capacity of individual selling is to push, and publicizing plays a draw work.

These two techniques are utilized together and supported by showcasing research, item advancement, improvement, estimating, vendor association, collaboration, and the actual appropriation of products themselves.

To be successful, selling should be gone before by a few promoting exercises like necessities evaluation, showcasing research, item improvement, valuing, and circulation.

In the event that the advertiser works really hard of recognizing shopper needs, creating proper items, and estimating, appropriating, and advancing them successfully, these items will sell without any problem.

Showcasing in view of hard-selling conveys high dangers since a buyer isn't content with the item will revile it to eleven colleagues, and it will duplicate to a similar rate by those; terrible news voyages quick.

One fascinating point to make reference to here is that accentuation is given on showcasing research, not on statistical surveying. Other than its application in the substantial merchandise business, the selling idea is additionally drilled in not-for-profit regions, like asset raisers, school confirmations workplaces, and ideological groups.

Example of a Selling Concept:

Have you ever seen an internet or television advertising that you couldn't seem to get away from? The Selling Concept is now in use.

Almost every business eventually succumbs to this philosophy. Ads for "Mountain Dew" are difficult to ignore. It's debatable whether people like Mountain Dew or not, but PepsiCo is clearly promoting it through advertisements.

The selling principle is used to almost all soft drinks and soda drinks. These beverages have no health advantages and may even be harmful to your health; you can easily replace them with water (the most available substances on the earth).

Soft drink firms are well aware of this, and they advertise 24 hours a day, seven days a week, for millions of dollars.

Marketing Concept –

The promoting idea holds-"accomplishing hierarchical objectives relies upon knowing the requirements and needs of target advertises and conveying the ideal fulfillments better than contenders do."

Here promoting the executives takes a "client first" approach. Under the advertising idea, client concentration and worth are the courses to accomplish deals and benefits.

The promoting idea is a client focused "sense and answers" reasoning. The occupation isn't to track down the right clients for your item however to track down your clients' right items.

The advertising idea and the selling ideas are two outrageous ideas and not the same as one another.

At the point when organizations began accomplishing the capacity to create in abundance of existing interest, leaders began understanding the need to reappraise showcasing in business activities. They likewise began perceiving the massive changes on the lookout, in the area of innovation, and how to reach and speak with business sectors. These progressions had prompted the development of the "promoting idea," which, generally, is a way of thinking of the board.

The advertising idea can be appeared differently in relation to prior ideas concerning the standards of direction. In the prior ideas, merchandise would be brought to the market in the desire for tracking down clients. Going against the norm, the promoting idea proposes that advertising begins with the clients and works back to the development of wanted items in the perfect sums and with the right particulars.

As Joseph C. According to seibert, *"showcasing the executives doesn't have the goal of making clients to the extent that it is answerable for making or building markets. The direction is coordinated toward making markets instead of making items."*

As per Philip Kotler, the showcasing idea holds that the way to accomplishing hierarchical objectives comprises of being more successful than rivals in coordinating advertising exercises toward deciding and fulfilling the requirements and needs of target showcases, or deciding the necessities and needs of target showcases and conveying the ideal fulfillments more really and effectively than contenders.

This definition proposes that advertising begins with the market, centers consideration around clients' requirements, and achieves benefit through consumer loyalty with facilitated promoting.

Under this way of thinking, the advertiser's most memorable assignment is to distinguish the necessities and needs of his possibility, then ought to work in reverse through the exchange channel and actual appropriation and proceed with this opposite course past the delivery entryway, past the creation and mechanical production system, right to the planning phases and examination labs. Under this idea, all parts of organization activities are pointed toward fulfilling clients' needs and wants.

One significant highlight be referenced here is that an organization's activity is likewise impacted by the organization's general objective or goal. For instance, an organization may be pointed toward fulfilling purchasers' needs and wants, however its general goal may be to expand the benefit volume.

The above discussion suggests that the marketing concept is based on four main pillars,

1. market focus,
2. customer orientation,
3. coordinated marketing, and
4. profitability.

The above bases propose one more clear meaning of the advertising idea set forward by W. J. Stanton. As per him, "in its fullest sense, the showcasing idea is a business reasoning that expresses that clients' need fulfillment is the monetary and social legitimization of an organization's presence.

Thusly, all organization exercises underway, designing, and money, as well as in showcasing, should be committed first to figuring out what the clients' needs are and afterward to fulfilling those needs while as yet creating a sensible gain."

- **Pillar 1 of the Marketing Concept - Market Focus**

The showcasing idea proposes that an organization ought to concentrate on promoting as opposed to creation and selling. In the present different market, it isn't practical for an organization to work effectively in each market and fulfill its necessities.

In this way, it is great for an organization to feature its regard for a specific fragment (s) of the all out heterogeneous market.

- **Pillar 2 of the Marketing Concept - Customer Orientation**

Zeroing in on a specific market doesn't ensure an organization's outcome in the commercial centre. What is required for progress is client direction, i.e., cautiously characterizing client needs according to clients' perspectives. An organization can do this with statistical surveying, and consequently, the job of statistical surveying assumes a prevailing part in promoting idea situated organizations.

Client direction is significant as in an organization's future and progress rely upon the clients. Clients can be new and old. An organization should hold its old clients since drawing in new clients is truly challenging and expensive.

A fulfilled client will purchase over and over, and he/she will talk high about the organization, which will build the organization's picture and assist with drawing in new clients.

Subsequently, an organization must be client situated, i.e., to distinguish their requirements and needs and sensibly fulfill those.

To guarantee consumer loyalty, an organization ought to empower client grumblings, since it is seen from various examinations that 96% of despondent clients never inform the organization concerning their disappointment. Subsequently, the organization ought to step up from its own to urge clients to whine.

It is likewise indispensable for an organization since analysis from a disappointed client can cause the company's ruination. Then again, an organization can get very supportive creative thoughts from its clients' objections.

It can likewise further develop its item quality and administration level assuming it knows what clients really care about. In this manner it might build the quantity of faithful clients and benefit volume.

- **Pillar 3 of the Marketing Concept - Coordinated Marketing**

The showcasing idea is an all out big business idea. To find lasting success, all promoting capacities should be facilitated among themselves, and second, advertising itself should be all around composed with different offices. An organization oversaw under the promoting idea should design, sort out, direction, and control its whole situation as one framework coordinated toward accomplishing a solitary arrangement of targets relevant to the complete association.

There are clear explanations for organizing advertising capacities among themselves, and the principal reason is to take out struggle. For instance, in the event that promoting capacities are not facilitated among themselves, the salesforce could vigorously condemn showcasing individuals for setting an exceptionally high deals target.

The explanation for coordination with different divisions is that advertising can't work in disengagement. On the off chance that representatives of different divisions don't perceive what they mean for consumer loyalty, the showcasing office can't the only one give it.

To showcase situated, an organization is to complete both inside and outer promoting.

Inner showcasing implies effectively recruiting, preparing, and inspiring representatives to work well for the clients and fulfill them.

Inside showcasing is to be done first in light of the fact that except if an organization isn't prepared to give consumer loyalty, it can't go for outside promoting. Under the promoting idea, showcasing turns into the essential persuading force for the whole firm.

The situation with advertising individuals likewise changes, and promoting comes in the closer view of the organization activity. The whole organization attempts to create, production, and sell an item according to the promoting point of view. With respect to business we are in, the organization, for instance, says, "we sell magnificence and trust rather than we sell beauty care products."

The significance of various degrees of the board likewise changes with the reception of the promoting idea. Clients come at the highest point of the association and afterward come bleeding edge individuals who meet, serve, and fulfill clients.

Center administration is there to help cutting edge individuals so they can more readily serve the clients, and top administration stays at the base to help center administration with the goal that they can actually and proficiently offer help to the forefront individuals.

- **Pillar 4 of the Marketing Concept - Profitability**

The finish of the showcasing idea is to create gains through consumer loyalty. This recommends that benefit is to be made by fulfilling clients' requirements.

As clients' necessities are changing step by step, a showcasing idea situated organization needs to consider and adjust its item, administration, and exercises with the adjustment of requirements and fulfill clients better than its rivals due to procure benefit over the long haul.

Example of a Marketing Concept:

The marketing concept is followed by restaurants and entrepreneurs. They make an effort to comprehend the customer in order to provide the ideal product or service possible, which is superior to the competitors.

The best example is the 'Dollar Shave Club.' They revolutionised the men's grooming industry. They've realised that customers are dissatisfied with their past grooming goods and prices.

Whereas other companies' grooming products can cost hundreds of dollars for a month's supply. The 'Dollar Shave Club' costs a few dollars a month for higher-quality goods and home delivery.

Difference between Selling Concept and Marketing Concept:

Theodore Levitt of Harvard drew an insightful differentiation between the selling and showcasing ideas. As per him, "selling centres around the requirements of the merchant; promoting on the necessities of the purchaser.

Selling is distracted with the vender's need to change over his item into cash; promoting with fulfilling the requirements of the client using the item and with the entire group of things related with making, conveying lastly consuming it."

You realize that the advertising idea depends on four support points, viz., target market, client needs, coordinated showcasing, and productivity. It takes an outside-inside view.

Then again, the selling idea takes an inside-outside viewpoint (see the figure underneath).

The promoting idea begins with a clear cut market, centres around client needs, facilitates every one of the exercises that will influence clients, and produce benefits by fulfilling clients.

Selling idea arranged organizations begin arranging with the industrial facility, centres around the organization's current items, and attempts weighty selling and elevating to deliver productive deals.

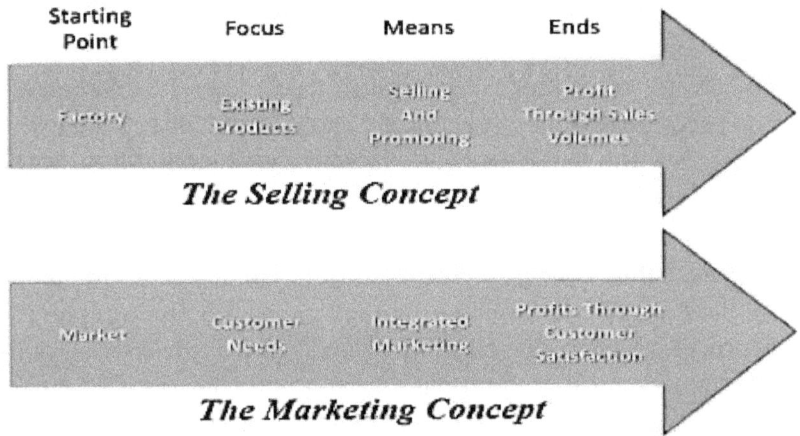

Source: iEduNote

Societal Marketing Concept –

Cultural advertising idea questions whether the unadulterated showcasing idea neglects potential struggles between shopper short-run needs and buyer long-run government assistance.

The cultural showcasing idea holds "promoting procedure ought to convey worth to clients in a manner that keeps up with or further develops both the shopper's and society's prosperity."

It calls for manageable advertising, socially and naturally dependable showcasing that meets customers' and organizations' current necessities while additionally saving or upgrading people in the future's capacity to address their issues.

The Societal Marketing Concept puts human government assistance on top before benefits and fulfilling the needs.

The unnatural weather change signal for an emergency response is pushed, and a disclosure is expected to utilize our assets. So organizations are gradually either completely or somewhat attempting to carry out the cultural advertising idea.

This is essentially an administration direction that holds that the critical undertaking of the firm is to decide the requirements and needs of target markets and to adjust the association to convey the ideal fulfillments more proficiently and successfully than rivals in a manner jam and improves the prosperity of the customers specifically and the general public overall.

It calls upon advertisers to adjust three contemplations in setting their showcasing arrangements: organization benefits, buyer need fulfilment and public interest.

Organizations might take on the cultural promoting idea in the event that it doesn't bring about cutthroat impediment or misfortune in the organization's benefit. It is on the grounds that any contemporary organization's essential objective is to keep its clients cheerful and create gains through serving and fulfilling clients.

Example of Social Marketing Concept:

While huge firms occasionally establish initiatives or products that assist society, it is difficult to find a company that is entirely committed to social responsibility.

Adidas is doing a fantastic job in continuing to back Colin Kaepernick despite pressure from a variety of sources. With electric automobiles and solar roof panels/tiles, Tesla plans to make a strong push for green energy.

Source: iEduNote

What are the many components of the marketing mix, and what role do they play in marketing?

The marketing mix refers to the four Ps of marketing: product, pricing, location, and promotion. These are the most important factors in marketing a product or service, and they interact heavily. One way to approach a holistic marketing plan is to consider all of these factors.

In terms of marketing concepts, what is the marketing mix?

As part of a comprehensive marketing plan, a marketing mix encompasses many areas of concentration. The term is frequently used to allude to the four Ps of marketing: product, price, placement, and promotion. Instead of focusing on a single message, effective marketing covers a wide range of topics.

The Marketing Mix 5 P's is a huge instrument to help you select and come up with the right showcasing systems for your business. It compels you to contemplate which region of your business you can change or enhance, to assist you with addressing the necessities of your objective market, add esteem and separate your item or administration from your rivals. The 5 regions you really want to come to conclusions about are:

PRODUCT, PRICE, PROMOTION, PLACE AND PEOPLE.

Albeit the 5 Ps are fairly controllable, they are generally dependent upon your inside and outer promoting conditions. Peruse on to figure out more about every one of the Ps.

PRODUCT/SERVICE -

The item or administration component alludes to what you are presenting overall to your clients. Item choices incorporate usefulness, marking, bundling, administration, quality, appearance and guarantee terms.

While pondering your item think about the key highlights, benefits, and necessities and needs of clients. For instance, in the event that you are a food maker, you might choose to add a few new flavours to expand your reach.

PRICE -

The cost component alludes to the manner in which you set costs for your items or administrations. It ought to incorporate every one of the parts that make up your general expense, including the promoted value, any limits, deals, credit terms or other installment courses of action.

Your valuing will likewise rely upon your organizations position on the lookout, for instance, in the event that you promote your business as a financial plan vehicle rental help, your evaluating ought to mirror that decision. Or on the other hand on the off chance that you are an exceptional food item, your cost ought to be at a higher cost than normal to lesser quality items to mirror the better bundling and nature of fixings you offer.

PROMOTION -

Advancement alludes to every one of the exercises and strategies you use to advance your items/administrations to your objective market. It incorporates deals, advertising, direct promoting, publicizing, sponsorship and web-based entertainment.

Since advancement expenses can be significant, it is reasonable to direct a profit from venture examination (ROI) while pursuing advancement choices. You, right off the bat, need to lay out who your objective market is, what media do they consume, what the expense of that media will be, the number of additional deals you that need to cover your speculation and how you will accumulate the data that shows how the advancement has functioned.

PLACE -

The spot component alludes to how you get your item or administration to your clients with perfect timing, at the ideal locations, and in the right amount. It incorporates dispersion channels (for example by means of a shopfront, on the web or a merchant), area, strategies, administration levels and market inclusion.

For instance, on the off chance that you're considering growing your business on the web, you'll have to ponder how your clients utilize the web, assuming they would feel happy with buying your merchandise on the web and on the off chance that they might want to pay transport costs for your items.

In the event that you're hoping to develop your business, you should seriously think about changing or extending the manner in which you sell your items and administrations. For instance, on the off chance that you're a homewares merchant, you could ponder setting up another store in an alternate area or offering establishments.

PEOPLE –

Individual component alludes to your clients, yourself and your staff. You want to think about both your staff and clients assuming you're considering developing your business. It incorporates understanding what your client's necessities and needs are, setting targets and estimating your client's care levels with the goal that you draw in and keep steadfast clients.

You'll likewise have to consider staff preparation so they bring the abilities to the table for the best insight and meet client assumptions.

Sources of finance:

Equity, debt, debentures, retained earnings, term loans, working capital loans, letter of credit, euro issue, venture investment, and other types of financing are available to businesses. This money are used in a variety of situations. They are categorised by time period, ownership and control, and generation source. Before deciding on a source of capital, it is best to assess it.

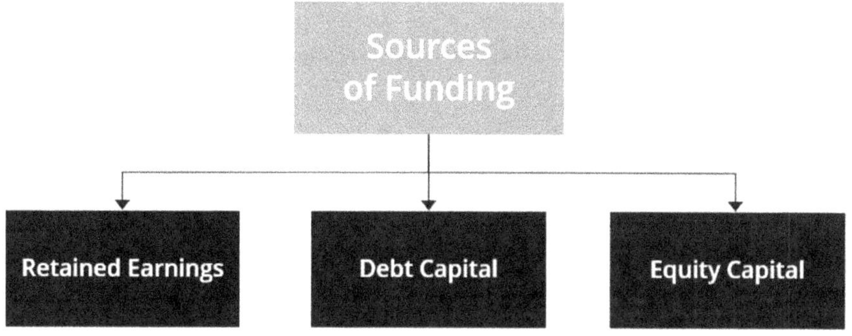

Source: Explorer Finance

Wellsprings of capital are the most explorable region, particularly for the business people who are going to begin another business. It is maybe the most difficult aspect of the relative multitude of endeavours. There are different capital sources we can arrange based on various boundaries.

Realizing that there are numerous choices to fund or capital an organization can look over. Picking the right source and the right blend of money is really difficult for each money chief. Choosing the right wellspring of money includes an inside and out investigation of each wellspring of assets. Examining and looking at the sources, it needs a comprehension of the relative multitude of qualities of the funding sources. There are numerous qualities based on which wellsprings of money are characterized.

Based on a time span, sources are named long haul, medium-term, and present moment. Possession and control characterize wellsprings of money into claimed and acquired capital. Inward sources and outside sources are the two wellsprings of age of capital. Every one of the sources have various attributes to suit various sorts of necessities. We should grasp them in a touch of profundity.

7 wellsprings of start-up funding (financing)

Tying up your resources in one place is never a decent business procedure. This is particularly obvious with regards to funding your new business. Not exclusively will differentiating your wellsprings of supporting permit your beginning up to all the more likely climate possible slumps, yet it will likewise work on your possibilities of getting the proper funding to meet your particular requirements.

Remember that financiers don't consider themselves to be your only wellspring of assets. What's more, showing that you've looked for or utilized different supporting choices exhibits to moneylenders that you're a proactive business visionary.

Whether you choose a bank credit, a private supporter, an administration award or a business hatchery, every one of these wellsprings of funding enjoys explicit benefits and disservices as well as measures they will use to assess your business.

Here is an outline of seven commonplace wellsprings of supporting for new businesses:

1. Individual speculation (Personal Investment) -

While beginning a business, your most memorable financial backer ought to act naturally — either with your own money or with insurance on your resources. This demonstrates to financial backers and brokers that you have a drawn out obligation to your task and that you are prepared to face challenges.

2. Love cash (Love Money) -

This is cash credited by a life partner, guardians, family or companions. Financial backers and investors thinks about this as "patient capital", which is cash that will be reimbursed later as your business benefits increment.

While getting love cash, you ought to know that:

- Loved ones seldom have a lot of capital
- They might need to have value in your business
- A business relationship with family or companions ought to never be messed with

3. Investment (Venture Capital) -

The principal thing to remember is that investment isn't really for all business people. Right from the beginning, you ought to know that financial speculators are searching for innovation-driven organizations and organizations with high-development potential in areas like data innovation, correspondences and biotechnology.

Financial speculators take a value position in the organization to assist it with completing a promising however higher gamble project. This includes surrendering a proprietorship or value in your business to an outer party. Investors likewise expect a solid profit from their speculation, frequently created when the business begins offering offers to people in general. Make certain to search for financial backers who carry important experience and information to your business.

BDC has a funding group that supports driving edge organizations decisively situated in a promising business sector. Like most other funding organizations, it engages in new businesses with high-development potential, liking to zero in on significant mediations when an organization needs a lot of support to get laid out in its market.

4. Holy messengers (Angels) -

Holy messengers are for the most part rich people or resigned organization chiefs who put straightforwardly in little firms possessed by others. They are many times pioneers in their own field who not just contribute their experience and organization of contacts yet additionally their specialized or potentially the board information. Holy messengers will generally fund the beginning phases of the business with interests in the request for $25,000 to $100,000. Institutional financial speculators lean toward bigger ventures, in the request for $1,000,000.

In return for taking a chance with their cash, they claim all authority to regulate the organization's administration rehearses. In substantial terms, this frequently includes a seat on the directorate and a confirmation of straightforwardness.

Holy messengers will generally stay under the radar. To meet them, you need to contact specific affiliations or search sites on holy messengers. The National Angel Capital Organization (NACO) is an umbrella association that helps construct limit with respect to Canadian private supporters. You can look at their part's catalogue for thoughts regarding who to contact in your district.

5. Business hatcheries (Business Incubators) -

Business hatcheries (or "gas pedals") for the most part centre around the super advanced area by offering help for new organizations in different transformative phases. Be that as it may, there are likewise neighbourhood financial advancement hatcheries, which are centred around regions like work creation, rejuvenation and facilitating and sharing administrations.

Ordinarily, hatcheries will welcome future organizations and other juvenile organizations to share their premises, as well as their regulatory, calculated and specialized assets. For instance, a hatchery could share the utilization of its research centres so another business can create and test its items all the more economically prior to starting creation.

By and large, the brooding stage can endure as long as two years. When the item is prepared, the business for the most part passes on the hatchery's premises to enter its modern creation stage and is all alone.

Organizations that get this sort of help frequently work inside cutting-edge areas like biotechnology, data innovation, media, or modern innovation.

6. Government awards and sponsorships (Government Grands and Subsidies) -

Government offices give funding, for example, awards and sponsorships that might be accessible to your business. The Canada Business Network site gives an exhaustive posting of different taxpayer-supported initiatives at the government and common levels.

Standards (Criteria)

Getting awards can be extreme. There might be areas of strength and the rules for grants are frequently rigid. By and large, most awards expect you to match the assets you are being given and this sum changes incredibly, contingent upon the granter. For instance, an examination award might expect you to see as just 40% of the all-out cost.

By and large, you should give:

- A point-by-point project portrayal
- A clarification of the advantages of your venture
- A nitty gritty work plan with full expenses
- Subtleties of significant experience and foundation on key directors
- Finished application structures when suitable

Most analysts will evaluate your proposition in light of the accompanying standards:

- Importance
- Approach
- Advancement
- Evaluation of mastery
- Need for the award

A portion of the trouble spots where competitors neglect to get awards include:

- The exploration/work isn't pertinent
- Ineligible geographic area
- Candidates neglect to convey the importance of their thoughts
- The proposition doesn't give areas of strength for a
- The exploration plan is unfocused
- There is an unreasonable measure of work
- Reserves are not coordinated

7. Bank credits (Bank Loans) -

Bank credits are the most regularly involved wellspring of financing for little and medium-sized organizations. Consider the way that all banks offer various benefits, whether it's customized administration or redid reimbursement. It's really smart to search around and track down the bank that meets your particular necessities.

As a general rule, you ought to realize financiers are searching for organizations with a sound history and that have incredible credit. Really smart isn't sufficient; it must be upheld with a strong field-tested strategy. Fire up credits will likewise ordinarily require an individual assurance from the business visionaries.

BDC offers fire up supporting to business visionaries in the beginning up stage or initial a year of deals. You may likewise have the option to defer the important instalments for as long as a year.

What is limited scale businesses (small scale industries)?

Limited scope Industries (SSI) are those businesses where the assembling, creation and delivering of administrations are done on a little or small size. These enterprises make a one-time interest in hardware, plant, and gear, yet it doesn't surpass Rs.10 crore and yearly turnover doesn't surpass Rs.50 crore

What efforts has been made by the Government for the development of small scale industries in India?

Government Policies for Development and Promotion of Small-Scale Industries in India

- Industrial Policy Resolution (IPR) 1948.
- Industrial Policy Resolution (IPR) 1956.
- Industrial Policy Resolution (IPR) 1977.
- Industrial Policy Resolution (IPR) 1980.
- Industrial Policy Resolution (IPR) 1990.

The various types of help extended by different support agencies of the government. Let us discuss them in detail.

1. Credit Support:

Of all the elements that go into a business, credit is perhaps the most crucial. The best of plans can come to naught if adequate finance is not available at the right time. MSEs need credit support not only for running the enterprise and operational requirements but also for diversification, modernization/up gradation of facilities, capacity expansion, etc.

This in turn led to a credit policy with the following components:

I. Priority Sector Lending: Credit to the MSE sector is ensured as part of the priority sector lending by banks. Banks are required to compulsorily ensure that a specified percentage (currently 40% for domestic commercial banks and 32% for foreign banks) of their overall lending is made to priority sectors as classified by the government. These sectors include agriculture, small enterprises, retail trade, etc.

II. Institutional Arrangement: SIDBI is the principal financial institution for promotion, financing, and development of the MSE sector. Apart from extending financial assistance to the sector, it coordinates the functions of institutions engaged in similar activities. State financial corporations (SFCs) and twin-function state industrial development corporations (SEDCs) at the state level are the main sources of long-term finance for the MSE sector. With the liberalization of the Indian economy, greater emphasis was placed on meeting the credit needs of MSEs. This was manifest through the following initiatives:

a. Earmarking of credit for micro enterprises within overall lending to micro and small enterprises.

b. Opening of specialized SME branches.

c. Enhancement in the limit for computation of the aggregate working capital requirements on the basis of minimum 20% of the projected annual turnover.

d. Enhancement of composite loan to Rs.1 crore (Rs.10 million).

e. No collateral security for loans up to Rs.5 lakh (Rs.0.5 million). Banks may on the basis of good track record and financial position of the units, increase the limit of dispensation of collateral requirement for loans up to Rs.25 lakh (2.5 million).

2. Marketing Support:

In today's world, marketing is much more than mere selling. Small enterprises can hardly match the advertising might or distribution reach of a large corporation. In India, small units sell best in limited or neighbourhood markets or when they are meeting a low volume specialized demand which no large player can effectively cater to.

The government agencies under marketing support provide the following types of help to SSIs:

I. Subcontracting exchanges – These exchanges enlist SSIs and identify items which can be supplied to public sector undertakings.

II. Marketing development assistance scheme – The government reimburses 60% of the expenditure incurred by SSI delegations that visit foreign countries for the purpose of exploiting marketing possibilities.

III. Training programmes for export packaging – Exporters are provided information on the latest packaging standards and techniques in order to boost exports.

IV. Organizing exhibitions and international trade fairs – Exhibitions and international trade fairs are organized abroad by the India Trade Promotion Organization. All expenses for SSIs on space charges, display, shipment, insurance, handling and clearance, publicity, etc. are borne by the government.

3. Entrepreneurship Development:

Beginning with psychological de-freezing and achievement motivation techniques, knowledge is imparted to participants on the scope and potential of different items, which can be manufactured in a small-scale industry, its technical feasibility, economic viability and commercial prospects as a self-employment venture. Efforts are directed not only to inform but to enable them to determine and identify all these themselves. Thus, they are led towards an entrepreneurial decision of product browsing and identification.

4. Technology Upgradation:

Small enterprises are regarded for their labour intensity and the capability to work with local resources. In the past, this has often led to less emphasis on technology. Run-of-the-mill coupled with functional packaging and inadequate, finishing have at times led to small sector products being labelled as being substandard. This has a cascading impact on competitiveness.

While sourcing technology, small businesses need to concentrate on the essential issues discussed below:

- **Information about Technology:** For small units, information about technology options is often through word of mouth or from a visit to an advanced unit. Only a few have access to technical literature, professional, journals or information about new product launches. In India, much of this is changing. With the advent of Internet, new vistas are opening up through electronic journals, catalogue downloads and advanced search facilities.

- **II. Actual Procurement of Technology:** Even with information, barriers to import of technology, technology transfer issues, vendor capability, after-sales support, import procedures impede procurement. In India, the Asia Pacific Centre for Transfer of Technology promotes match-making between buyer and seller and facilitates procurement through escort services. Encouragement to import of capital goods has also helped matters.

  III. Finance for Technology Upgradation: Small enterprises look to external sources of funding for upgrading technology as withdrawing money from business entails its own costs. In India, a technology upgradation and modernization fund and a hire-purchase scheme attempt to meet this requirement. These are, however, funds at normal lending costs. A new scheme called credit linked capital subsidy scheme for technology upgradation in small industries has been put into place to reduce the cost of funds.

Government Policy # Establishment of Small Industries Development Bank of India (SIDBI):

Independent venture area finds it hard to raise advances. Consequently, the Governments' strategy accommodates a special treatment, in regard of monetary help to private company.

In that capacity, 10% of absolute credit to be progressed by open area banks ought to go to limited scope specialty units.

Be that as it may, there has been no exceptional assistance to the limited scale area; as this arrangement is somewhat lacking.

A huge improvement in the field of stretching out extraordinary monetary help to the private venture has been made with the foundation of SIDBI; which is the chief establishment for the advancement, supporting and advancement of private company in India.

SIDBI has been framed for satisfying the well established need of the little area for a different bank to provide food solely to its requirements.

SIDBI was laid out in 1989 under the outright responsibility for Industrial Development Bank of India. It began working with impact from April 2, 1990.

The Mall Industries Development Bank of India (SIDBI) is a national organisation that promotes and finances the growth of micro, small, and medium-sized enterprises (MSMEs), primarily in the manufacturing and service sectors. SIDBI also supports national climate action plans and has taken initiatives to promote responsible business practises in the MSMEs sector, such as sustainable financing, energy efficiency, and cleaner production, through both financial and nonfinancial support.

References

- Peneder, M. (2009). The meaning of entrepreneurship: A modular concept. *Journal of Industry, Competition, and Trade, 9*(2), 77-99.
- (Pahuja, A., & Sanjeev, R. (2015). Introduction to Entrepreneurship.*Available at SSRN 2761878.*)
- Sikalieh, D., Mokaya, S. O., & Namusonge, M. (2012). The concept of entrepreneurship; in pursuit of a universally acceptable definition.
- Pittaway, Luke. (2005). Philosophies in Entrepreneurship: A Focus on Economic Theories. *Journal of Industry* Philosophies in Entrepreneurship: A Focus on Economic Theories 10.1108/13552550510598790
- Meyer, N., & de Jongh, J. (2018). The importance of entrepreneurship as a contributing factor to economic growth and development: The case of selected European countries. *Journal of Economics and Behavioural Studies, 10*(4 (J)), 287-299.
- Germain, O., & Aubry, M. (2019). Exploring processual and critical avenues at the crossroad of entrepreneurship and project management. International Journal of Managing Projects in Business.
- Heerkens, G. R. (2002). Project management. McGraw Hill Professional.
- Sears, S. K., Sears, G. A., Clough, R. H., Rounds, J. L., & Segner, R. O. (2015). Construction project management. John Wiley & Sons.
- Monden, Y., & Hamada, K. (1991). Target costing and kaizen costing in Japanese automobile companies. Journal of Management Accounting Research, 3(1), 16-34.
- Williams, A. R. T., Van der Wiele, A., & Dale, B. G. (1999). Quality costing: a management review. International Journal of Management Reviews, 1(4), 441-460.
- Borden, N. H. (1964). The concept of the marketing mix. Journal of advertising research, 4(2), 2-7.
- Goi, C. L. (2009). A review of marketing mix: 4Ps or more. International journal of marketing studies, 1(1), 2-15.Goi, C. L. (2009). A review of marketing mix: 4Ps or more. International journal of marketing studies, 1(1), 2-15.
- Newell, S. (2005). Recruitment and selection. Managing human resources: Personnel management in transition, 115-147.

- Hamza, P. A., Othman, B. J., Gardi, B., Sorguli, S., Aziz, H. M., Ahmed, S. A., ... & Anwar, G. (2021). Recruitment and selection: The relationship between recruitment and selection with organizational performance. International Journal of Engineering, Business and Management, 5(3), 1-13.
- Rao, U. A., & Ram, C. S. Effective Implementation of Wage and Salary Administration. Editor's Preface, 1.
- Bhatia, S. K. (2003). New Compensation Management in Changing Environment: Managerial Remuneration and Wage & Salary Administration: a Professional Manual. Deep and Deep Publications.
- Prasad, V. N. (2008). Small Service Enterprises Need Government's Interventions. SEDME (Small Enterprises Development, Management & Extension Journal), 35(3), 9-15.
- Rajan, S., & Panicker, S. The Role of Risk and Competition in Women MSME's-Literature Review and Implications.
- Ramanujam, V., & Murgesh, M. S. (2016). GROWTH AND PERFORMANCE OF MICRO, SMALL AND MEDIUM ENTERPRISES IN INDIA. Journal of Management, 186.
- https://saylordotorg.github.io/text_the-sustainable-business-case-book/s09-04-conclusion.html
- https://www.intechopen.com/books/entrepreneurship-development-tendencies-and-empirical-approach/entrepreneurs-and-growth-an-option-obligation-or-obsession
- https://byjus.com/commerce/what-is-entrepreneurship/
- https://www.vedantu.com/commerce/concepts-and-characteristics-of-entrepreneurship
- https://www.googlesir.com/nature-and-characteristics-of-entrepreneurship/
- https://commercemates.com/nature-and-characteristics-of-entrepreneurship/
- https://www.indeed.com/career-advice/career-development/why-are-human-resources-important
- https://talentedge.com/articles/six-main-functions-human-resource-management/